Ephraidge A. T. Rinombota

SPO
2/86   27 JUN 90

COMPUTER SECURITY

A HANDBOOK FOR MANAGEMENT

LEONARD H FINE

Published in Association with the
Irish Management Institute

HEINEMANN : LONDON

William Heinemann Ltd
10 Upper Grosvenor Street, London W1X 9PA
LONDON MELBOURNE TORONTO
JOHANNESBURG AUCKLAND

First published 1983
© Leonard H. Fine 1983

434 90578 X

Printed in Great Britain by
Richard Clay (The Chaucer Press) Ltd
Bungay, Suffolk

CONTENTS

Chapter 1 **A New Approach to Computer Security:**
          The Total Security Concept   1
1.   DEMANDS FOR ENHANCED COMPUTER SECURITY   1
    1.1   Concentration of Processing Larger and More Complex
          Applications   2
    1.2   Dependence upon Key Personnel   2
    1.3   Disappearance of Traditional Controls   3
    1.4   Strikes, Urban Terrorism and Unrest   4
    ·1.5   Greater Supplier Awareness   4
2.   TRADITIONAL APPROACHES TO COMPUTER SECURITY   4
3.   THE TOTAL COMPUTER SECURITY CONCEPT   5
4.   SUMMARY   7

PART 1: MANAGEMENT ELEMENTS

Chapter 2 **Defining a Computer Security Policy**   11
1.   LIMITATIONS OF SECURITY   11
2.   MATCHING SECURITY MEASURES WITH RISK LEVELS   11
3.   QUANTIFYING COMPUTER SECURITY RISKS   12
    3.1   Broadly Classifying Installations   12
    3.2   Identifying High, Medium and Low Risk Applications   13
          3.2.1   Step One: List Applications in Order of Risk   14
          3.2.2   Step Two: Quantification of Risk   14
          3.2.3   Step Three: Obtaining Consensus on Risk Levels   15
    3.3   Evaluating Security Measures   15
    3.4   Cost of Justifying Security Measures   15
4.   OBTAINING COMMITMENT TO THE SECURITY POLICY   16
5.   SUMMARY   17

Chapter 3   Organisation and Division of Responsibility   18
1.   DIVISION OF RESPONSIBILITY   18
2.   SYSTEMS OF INTERNAL CONTROL   19
3.   ASSIGNING RESPONSIBILITY FOR SECURITY   20
4.   SUCCESSION TO KEY PERSONNEL   21
5.   SUMMARY   21

Chapter 4   Physical and Fire Security   22
1.   LOCATION AND CONSTRUCTION OF THE COMPUTER
     FACILITY   22
     1.1   Location   22
     1.2   Construction   23
     1.3   Layout   23
2.   AIR-CONDITIONING   23
3.   POWER SUPPLY   24
4.   FLOOD RISK   24
5.   ACCESS   25
     5.1   Controls over Access During Different Times of the Day or
           Night   25
     5.2   Access by Third Parties   25
     5.3   Structure and Layout of the Reception Area   25
     5.4   Burglar Alarms and Proofing   26
     5.5   Card-Keys and Badges   26
6.   FIRE DETECTION   26
7.   FIRE PROTECTION   27
8.   FIRE FIGHTING   28
9.   HOUSEKEEPING   28
10. SUMMARY   29

Chapter 5   Personnel Practices   30
1.   RECRUITMENT PRACTICES   30
     1.1   Reference Checking and Security Clearance   30
     1.2   Psychological Testing   31
     1.3   Medical Examinations   31
2.   PERFORMANCE APPRAISAL PROCEDURES   31
3.   LEAVE POLICY   32
4.   JOB ROTATION   32
5.   PERSONNEL ATTITUDE EVALUATION   33
6.   SUMMARY   33

Chapter 6   Insurance   34
1. TRADITIONAL PROBLEMS   34
2. INSURANCE RISK AREAS   35
   2.1   Environment   35
   2.2   Equipment   35
     2.2.1   Responsibility for Insurance   35
     2.2.2   Risks to be Covered   36
   2.3   Software and Data   37
     2.3.1   Definitions   37
     2.3.2   Insurance against Loss or Damage   37
     2.3.3   Software   37
   2.4   Business Interruption and Recovery   38
     2.4.1   Assessment of Consequences 38
     2.4.2   Cost Effects of Interruption   39
   2.5   Personnel   39
     2.5.1   Damage Caused by Personnel 39
     2.5.2   Injury to Personnel   39
     2.5.3   Dishonest Actions by Personnel   39
   2.6   Third Party Liabilities   39
3. SPECIALISED INSURANCE SERVICES   40
4. MONITORING CHANGING RISKS   40
5. SUMMARY   40

PART 2: TECHNICAL AND PROCEDURAL ELEMENTS
Chapter 7   Systems Security   45
1. SCOPE OF THE TERM   45
2. HARDWARE   45
3. SOFTWARE   45
4. NETWORKS   47
5. TERMINALS   47
6. PERFORMANCE MONITORING   48
7. SUMMARY   48

Chapter 8   Application Security   49
1. SCOPE   49
2. THE COMMON FLAW: THE CONNECTION BETWEEN THE COMPUTER AND THE USER   49

3.   USER CONTROLS   50
4.   COMPUTER PROCESSING CONTROLS AND FILE SECURITY   51
     4.1   Computer Processing Controls   51
     4.2   File Security   51
           4.2.1   Security Copies Stored at a Remote Location   51
           4.2.2   File Identification and Control   52
           4.2.3   File Accuracy   52
           4.2.4   Physical Access to Files   52
5.   REGULAR APPLICATION CONTROLS REVIEW   52
6.   SUMMARY   53

Chapter 9   Systems Programming and Operating Standards   54
1.   SYSTEMS AND PROGRAMMING STANDARDS   56
     1.1   Long Term: Security and Computer Planning   56
     1.2   Short Term: Application Quality Assurance   57
           1.2.1   Software and Hardware Security   57
           1.2.2   Application Controls   57
           1.2.3   Work Methods and Supervision   58
           1.2.4   Documentation   59
2.   OPERATIONS   60
3.   SUMMARY   60

Chapter 10   The Role of Internal and External Auditors   61
1.   GENERAL AUDIT ROLES   61
     1.1   External Auditors   61
     1.2   Internal Auditors   61
2.   COMPUTER AUDIT ROLES AND SECURITY   62
     2.1   Scope of Internal Audit in Computer Security   63
     2.2   Liaison between Internal and External Auditors   63
     2.3   Role of Internal Audit in Development   63
     2.4   Role in Operational Systems   64
     2.5   Education and Training   64
3.   SUMMARY   65

Chapter 11   Disaster Recovery Planning and Testing   66
1.   TYPES OF DISASTER   67
2.   SCOPE OF DISASTER PLANNING   67
3.   APPLICATIONS IN THE COURSE OF DEVELOPMENT   68
4.   COMPLETED APPLICATIONS   68
     4.1   Systems and Programming   68

    4.2   Processing Operations   69
          4.2.1   Equipment   69
          4.2.2   Data and Files   69
          4.2.3   Stationery   70
          4.2.4   Procedures for Disaster   70
5.   DISASTER TESTS   71
     5.1   Scope of Disaster Tests   71
     5.2   Timing of Disaster Tests   71
     5.3   Form of Disaster Test   71
     5.4   Analysis of Impact   72
6.   SUMMARY   72

PART 3: IMPLEMENTATION

Chapter 12   Implementing Effective Computer Security   75
1.   DEFINING THE SCOPE OF COMPUTER SECURITY   75
2.   ESTABLISHING A COMPUTER SECURITY COMMITTEE   76
     2.1   Objectives   76
     2.2   Constitution   76
     2.3   Method of Operation   76
3.   REVIEW OF CURRENT SECURITY EFFECTIVENESS   77
4.   IMPLEMENTING SECURITY MEASURES   78
     4.1   Commitment   78
     4.2   Follow-through   79
     4.3   Policy   79
     4.4   Communications   80
     4.5   Security Management   80
     4.6   Elapsed Time to Implementation   81
     4.7   Priority of Security Activities   81
     4.8   Costs   81
          4.8.1   Physical Security   81
          4.8.2   Systems Auditability and Control   82
          4.8.3   Existing Applications   82
5.   COMPILE AN ACTION PLAN   83
6.   DISASTER PLANNING AND TESTS   83
7.   LONG-RANGE COMPUTER PLANNING AND SECURITY   83
8.   SUMMARY   83

Appendix 1 Computer Security Risk Inventory   84
Appendix 2 Computer Security Review   86
Appendix 3 Computer Security Review
            Extract of Checklist on Evidential Checks   88
Appendix 4 Case Study: Computer Security in a Small Installation   89
Appendix 5 Glossary of Computer Terms   93
Appendix 6 Further Reading   96

CHAPTER 1

A New Approach to Computer Security: The Total Security Concept

1. DEMANDS FOR ENHANCED COMPUTER SECURITY

For a number of years, the computer has been a good whipping-boy with sensational publicity being given to amusing and hair-raising experiences of computer use. An immediate consequence has been the multitude of articles and literature on the subject. In North America and Europe, government-sponsored research has been expanded, leading to the publication of many books and articles on computer abuse and security. Firms specialising in computer security consulting services have proliferated. In more than one case these firms are now headed by individuals with criminal records who have perpetrated theft or fraud in large computer installations.

It is the trimmings are removed it is clear that an important new area for management concern has developed: computer abuse or disaster flowing from theft, fraud, sabotage or disruption of computer activities. Computer security is still the subject of much inadequate consideration. Few of the books which have been written contain an overall framework to address this complex problem. Specific emphasis is thus placed on traditional areas such as physical and fire security. Many organisations which have addressed these areas then live in a fool's paradise of adequate security, when in reality the level of computer security is sub-standard and top management commitment to meaningful effectiveness is low. Awareness may be raised temporarily by a disaster or abuse of computer resources but routine effectiveness is at best sporadic. The typical attitudes are *'we are satisfied with our computer security'*, and *'that's not likely to happen here'*.

It is these elements which have prompted the writing of this monograph, which is a methodical attempt to provide an effective overall framework for computer security and guide-lines for computer users. Certain aspects such as computer auditing and insurance are covered as they constitute an integral part of a balanced approach to computer security. In these cases only the important facets are reviewed, as the book is not intended as a treatise on these specialist subjects.

Against this backdrop of computer security, which is generally superficial, there are a number of factors which have changed the environment in which computers are used, and enhanced the levels of security demanded:

- Concentration of processing and larger and more complex applications which form an integral part of the organisation.
- Dependence upon key personnel.
- Disappearance of traditional controls.
- Urban terrorism and unrest.
- Greater computer supplier awareness.

Each of these is now discussed in further detail.

1.1   Concentration of Processing Larger and More Complex Applications

Probably the main reason for greater computer risk is the increasing number of computer applications and the consequent concentration of information and processing. The increasing trend towards larger and more complex systems incorporating on-line and real-time processing, frequently with large and sophisticated data bases or files, is a further complication. The introduction of data base systems is becoming increasingly widespread and large quantitites of confidential data are stored in this way, e.g. credit bureaux, government departments.

In contrast to an organisation using manual record-keeping where records are diversified throughout the organisation, one with extensive computerisation has data and programs concentrated in the hands of a few individuals. As a consequence, the computerised organisation runs the risk of 'corporate amnesia' flowing from a computer disaster resulting in the protracted suspension of processing. The greater awareness of this risk and a few highly publicised disasters has led to increasing concern for computer security.

A medium-sized corporation making extensive use of computers was put into liquidation when its computer centre was hit by an aircraft which crashed into it. The high dependence on computerised activity and the loss of all computerised records left the organisation incapable of continuing its business activities.

1.2   Dependence upon Key Personnel

In addition to the risk exposure flowing from a disaster, there are a number of other implications. Probably the most important of these is the dependence on key individuals. While this situation exists in every function of an organisation, the relative youth of computer experience and the 'communication gap' between technical experts and line management creates unique problems.

The programmer at a large bank responsible for the development of the salary application, harboured a number of grievances. When he wrote the salary application he made provision that when his employment was terminated, the termination notice would initiate a series of secret routines in the application, which would lead to processing being aborted. It took the organisation some time to unravel the cause of the protracted disruption in processing. Dependence on this individual and difficulties in monitoring his work at a detailed level, enabled him to perpetrate this disaster.

The dependence upon key individuals, some of whom have a high level of technical proficiency, often places the organisation in the hands of a relatively few individuals. Software in particular is becoming increasingly complex and a person with technical knowledge of software and/or hardware and 'trapdoors' or weaknesses is invariably placed in a unique position of control. Knowledge of this type has led to a number of situations where organisations have been exposed to blackmail and extortion.

A software expert in a large concern manipulated programs and files through 'trapdoors'. As a result, he not only defrauded the company of substantial sums of money, but used considerable quantities of unauthorised computer time.

The threat is not limited to abuse of the type described. These specialist personnel often have unique and undocumented knowledge of modifications to, or the operation of, software. Supervision and control of their work is difficult as is the knowledge of what **will** work without the specialist skills of one of these 'boffins'.

1.3   Disappearance of Traditional Controls

The importance of technical skills is enhanced by the disappearance of traditional controls and audit traits in many installations. The communication gap between technical staff, line management and outsiders such as auditors already referred to, frequently causes difficulty in establishing the practical implications of this development in conventional commercial terms. A classical and widely publicised example of this was the Equity Funding case where a large number of insurance policies were fictitiously created, thereby enhancing the assets and profitability of the organisation.

The commication gap also extends to other experts such as security personnel. Security managers are rarely experts in computerisation. They have difficulty in applying their established security and risk evaluations to the computer activity.

A large manufacturing concern with extensive computerisation had relied on a security department to evaluate risk and establish the required security procedures. The security department completely skirted any aspects of computerisation with technical overtones. In this respect they were also discouraged by the computer personnel who felt that their flexibility might be restricted. As a result, there were major gaps in security. A key master file containing salary information was removed without authority and confidential information obtained on the organisation's remuneration practices.

Many of the large new applications omit traditional audit traits or hard copy (printed) controls for reasons of volume. The applications contain automatic checks to ensure the integrity of the data which is being processed. This major change in clerical control philosophy and the gaps in communications create completely different security situations.

1.4   Strikes, Urban Terrorism and Unrest
The present level of computer risk has also to be reviewed in the context of urban unrest and terrorism in many parts of the world. Installations in North America and Europe have been physically attacked. Sometimes, however, installations have been penetrated by internal personnel rather than by rioters. This insidious type of risk is potentially the source of greatest harm to an organisation. This risk alone creates a wide range of new threats which have to be responded to.

Internal attack by personnel in an organisation can take the form of a strike. This, while non-violent, can be as crippling as a physical attack. Strikes have occurred in major on-line installations in Scandinavia and Britain.

1.5   Greater Supplier Awareness
Finally, there has been increased supplier research and support in the security area. Until a few years ago this subject was not of major supplier concern, but an awareness of the risk exposure has forced all the suppliers to allocate substantial research budgets into computer security. As a result there has been an increasing flow of high quality literature to users. This has served to improve the structure of, and approach to, computer security. It has also heightened concern for the progressively reduced risk through a computer disaster.

2.   TRADITIONAL APPROACHES TO COMPUTER SECURITY
The developments outlined above have resulted in concern about, and action to, reduce vulnerability. Attention has traditionally been devoted to areas where visible results can be seen. As a result, the main areas of enhanced security, as mentioned earlier, have been:

1. Physical security embracing access and fire security.
2. Data and file security.

Consequently, few organisations can be visited today where there are not comprehensive access control procedures involving security officers and card-key control systems. Files are religiously copied and moved for storage in a remote location. Whilst these aspects are certainly elements of an overall approach to computer security, they do not alone create an environment which is adequate. Many organisations place almost blind dependence upon these elements for computer security.

A large defence installation had an extremely high level of computer security. The perimeter of the installation was protected by a double twelve foot security fence. The area between the perimeter and the installation was patrolled. Yet within the installation itself the staff of 250 security cleared personnel had virtually unlimited access to all aspects of the installation. While trust in personnel is obviously a key element, blind dependence upon it is unsatisfactory.

Another characteristic of this narrow perspective is that it is rare to find that a full and comprehensive review of security has been undertaken. Security awareness is generally initiated by top management concerned by some publicised breach of security. Alternatively, a minor incident arises within the organisation, or a call is received from a security consultant or salesman offering fire-proof safes, fire-fighting equipment, etc. The consequence is very much a 'flavour of the month' approach. This month it is fire-proof safes, next month a new access system, the month after fire-fighting equipment, and so on.

3. THE TOTAL COMPUTER SECURITY CONCEPT

The requirements are thus for a broad approach embracing a number of related issues in a methodical way. There are two major areas to be incorporated in such an approach:

1. Management issues.
2. Technical and procedural issues.

The key issues may be summarised as follows:

Management elements
   A defined computer security policy.
   Organisation and division of responsibility.
   Physical and fire security.
   Personnel practices.
   Insurance.

Technical and procedural elements
   Systems security (hardware and software, including networks and terminal systems).
   Applications security including data and file security.
   Systems, programming and operations standards.

Role of internal and external audit.

Disaster planning and testing.

Careful scrutiny of these areas will reveal that there is not one which, in its own right, is of exclusive importance. In a particular installation, one may be of greater consequence, and hence require greater emphasis. But excluding one of the areas will certainly leave gaps in security management and control. The approach developed which methodically embraces all of these areas is referred to as 'The Total Computer Security Concept' (TSC). The interlocking impact of this concept can best be illustrated in the figure below.

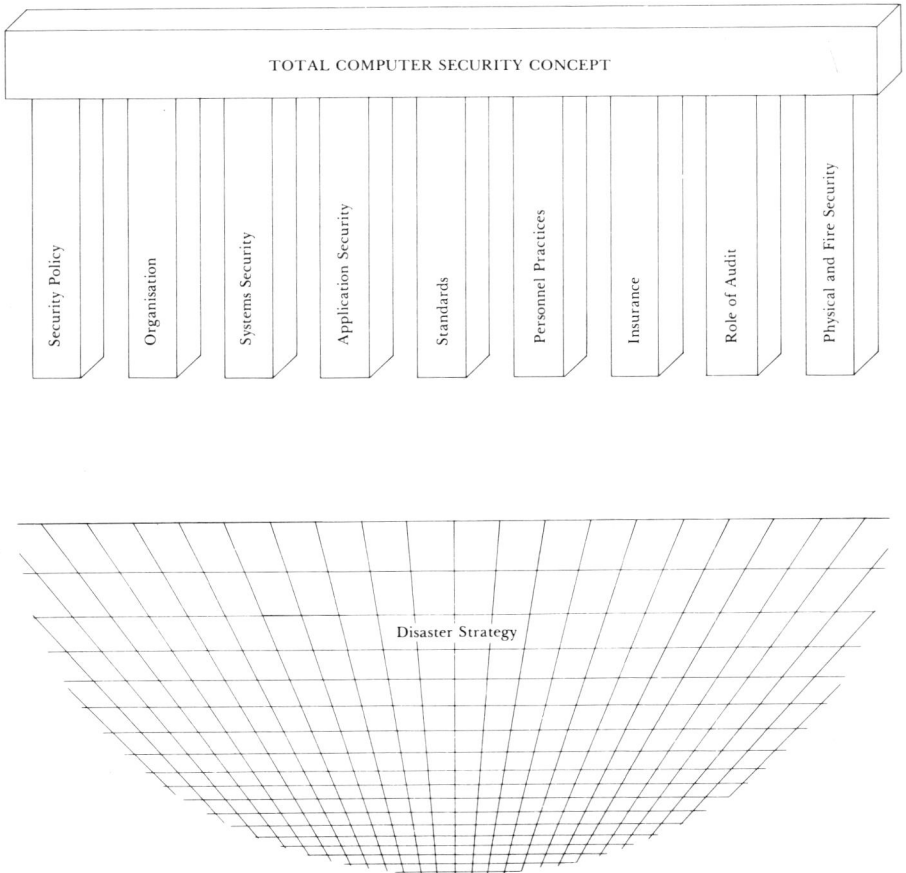

TOTAL COMPUTER SECURITY CONCEPT

Security Policy

Organisation

Systems Security

Application Security

Standards

Personnel Practices

Insurance

Role of Audit

Physical and Fire Security

Disaster Strategy

A concrete beam is supported by ten columns, each comprising one of the elements of the total security concept. The objective is that the columns should support the beam in a position which is horizontal to the ground. A weakness in any one of the columns will require that others are to be strengthened if the column is to be maintained parallel to the ground. Weaknesses in two or more columns will cause the beam to tilt and possibly break or fall. In this way it is clear that one cannot eliminate any one column or exclude it from consideration, as it will have an impact on the other areas. The beam and columns are on firm ground but there is a safety net to catch the beam in the event of a disaster. This is the disaster or contingency plan for the installation.

Each of these areas is now discussed in a separate chapter. This book is divided into three parts which correspond to the Total Security Concept.

Part 1: Management Elements of Computer Security.
Part 2: Technical and Procedural Elements of Computer Security.
Part 3: Implementation.

Part 3 is an essential part of any approach to computer security. Thus while it is an integral part of the TSC, it is dealt with in a separate section.

4.   SUMMARY
The increasing complexity and comprehensiveness of computerisation has led to the concentration of information in the hands of a few people. Traditional focus on security issues is on those that are 'visible', i.e. physical access, fire fighting and file security. Effective computer security requires re-evaluation of a broad number of issues which are outlined in the Total Security Concept.

PART I   MANAGEMENT ELEMENTS

DEFINING A COMPUTER SECURITY POLICY
ORGANISATION AND DIVISION OF
  RESPONSIBILITY
PHYSICAL AND FIRE SECURITY
PERSONNEL PRACTICES
INSURANCE

CHAPTER 2

Defining a Computer Security Policy

A prerequisite to any approach to computer security is defining a clear security policy. In most organisations this is ill-defined or non-existent. This chapter reviews the issues which will require consideration in defining a security policy and the elements of the approach to doing this.

1. LIMITATIONS OF SECURITY

In the final analysis security is dependent upon the integrity of the individuals in an organisation. There is no such thing as 100 per cent security and an organisation is dependent upon its personnel to achieve designated levels of security.

As is commonplace in other areas of management, it is generally possible to achieve certain minimum levels of security without large expenditure. Thereafter, the achievement of additional protection requires higher levels of expenditure frequently with diminishing returns. Economics always has a relevance and it is important to ensure that there is a sound cost/benefit relationship in addressing security measures, just as there is in any other area of management activity.

2. MATCHING SECURITY MEASURES WITH RISK LEVELS

Not every computer installation has the same security demands — some are higher than others. In assessing the degree of risk, it is important first to consider the types of risk to which the computer installations are exposed:

1. Accidents flowing from mismanagement or negligence.
2. Deliberate attack in the form of theft, fraud, sabotage or strikes.

Effective computer security should ensure the prevention and detection of an accident or attack, the existence of clearly defined measures to deal with a disaster when it occurs, and if there has been a disruption of processing, then the resuscitation thereof. Some computer installations and their applications are of high risk, with material impact to the organisation or the community if processing is disrupted for a protracted period. Others do not form a material or integral part of an organisation and can be easily backed up with manual procedures. It is clear, therefore, that there is little point in exaggerating the level of security procedures for low-risk situations; conversely, where there is high risk, equivalent protection must be provided. However, the quantification

11

of risk appears at first glance to be a subjective issue. This makes it difficult to express in normal commercial terms and, as a result, many organisations either avoid the problem or give up quantification prematurely.

3.   QUANTIFYING COMPUTER SECURITY RISKS

The quantification of computer security risk is probably the most important part of an organisation's approach to computer security. Unless risks are quantified, it will be difficult to justify at a subsequent stage the measures which have been identified as necessary. In fact, the absence of a quantified security policy is the primary reason for many worthwhile security recommendations not being accepted as cost-justified by top management.

There are a number of steps involved in quantifying security risks:

1. Broadly classifying installations in terms of high, medium or low risk.
2. Identifying those applications which constitute high risks.
3. Quantifying the impact of a protracted suspension of processing for high risk applications.
4. Formulating the measures necessary for an adequate level of security, i.e. commensurate with the risk levels.
5. Cost justifying security measures.

Each of these aspects is now discussed below.

3.1   Broadly Classifying Installations

The first step is broadly to assess whether the installation is high, medium or low risk. High risk installations have the following characteristics:

1. Data or programs which contain secret information which is in the national interest or which have a high competitive value in the market place.
2. A large potential financial loss to the community through a disaster or a widespread impact on members of the public.
3. Large potential loss to the organisation and consequentially a high potential threat to its survival.

All high risk installations will contain one or more of the above characteristics. It is therefore usually easy to identify high risk installations. Differentiating between medium and low risk ones is much more difficult. Practically speaking, it is rarely that important to do so and the real issue which emerges is the impact on the organisation's health or survival in the event of a protracted suspension in processing of, say, four to six weeks. Posing this question will typically classify installations as follows:

Medium risk applications are those where protracted disruption will cause great inconvenience and possibly incremental costs. However, little material loss will flow.

A good example in many corporations of a medium risk application is payroll. This is a time-critical application which is most important to the corporation. If pay is incorrect or late, large numbers of personnel will be aggrieved and work may be disrupted and large quantities of management time expended in resolving the consequent grievances. However, it is relatively easy to structure back-up procedures for payroll applications although sometimes incremental costs may be involved.

Low risk applications are those where a protracted processing has little material impact on the organisation in terms of costs or disruption. General ledger processing is frequently a good example of a low-risk application, although in today's competitive world the need for timely reporting may increase the risk levels. General ledger, while time-critical, will not permanently impair an organisation's health, even if processing is suspended for three to four weeks. Back-up is generally easy to arrange and is also low cost.

In order to expedite the risk classification process, it may be helpful to complete the computer security risk inventory contained in Appendix 1. This inventory should only be completed once the broad classification of risk described above has been completed. A review of the items marked 'YES' in the 'KEY ISSUE' column will give a useful perspective of the risk levels to which the organisation is exposed. Any items marked 'NO' in the 'ADEQUATE' column will point to items for action. Some organisations have taken the risk inventory one step further by attaching points to each item according to a waiting scale which they believe is appropriate to their organisation. By assigning, say, 100 points to all of the items of the inventory and then assessing needs in terms of high, medium or low risk for each item, a subjective allocation of points is derived for each element of the inventory. At the 100 point level, one has a high security installation, typically of a defence-type nature. Most large banks or organisations with high dependence levels on their computer will be ranked around the 90-95 level. Most commercial installations will be placed on the scale around the 60-75 level. Any ranking method of this type is at best subjective, but it does help to formulate a preliminary picture of the risk levels which are inherent in an installation.

3.2   Identifying High, Medium and Low Risk Applications

Even in a high security installation, not all of the applications can be classified as high risk. It is, therefore, necessary to now take the security analysis one step further and to identify those applications which constitute the greatest risk to the organisation and to rank them according to the importance of risk.

3.2.1   STEP ONE: LIST APPLICATIONS IN ORDER OF RISK

All applications should be listed in tabular form in what is assessed to be the descending order of risk importance. The following factors need to be listed for each application:

a. Application title or description.

b. Key programs and nature of risk, i.e.
   - Secrecy or national interest.
   - Competitive value in market place due to uniqueness of computations or scale and complexity.

c. File information, also annotated as to:
   - Secrecy or national interest.
   - Internal confidentiality or market value.
   - Level of risk, i.e. high, medium or low, and general assessment of the consequences of abuse or disaster.

Recording this information in a tabular form facilitates the preliminary discussion of risk amongst top management. It also expedites the identification of those applications on which the majority of effort should be focused.

3.2.2   STEP TWO: QUANTIFICATION OF RISK

This is extremely difficult but must be achieved — it requires perserverance. It is very similar in nature to the quantification of non-financial objectives in an organisation. Frequently the first reaction is that it is impossible, but after careful and detailed review, time-bound and measurable objectives are defined.

A medium-sized manufacturing and distribution concern, with a turnover in excess of £200 million per annum, identified its order-entry invoicing, debtors and stock control as a high risk application. Having done this, there was considerable difficulty in quantifying the impact of a protracted disruption in computer services. It was only after close consultation with the commercial management that the main consequence of such a disruption was agreed to be a likely loss in market share. This was quantified by the management as being of the order of 1-2 per cent with a value of between £10 million and £20 million.

Experience reveals that the most practical approach to this problem is to commence by interviewing all of the senior managers directly affected by a suspension in processing and to request them to quantify the impact of such a situation. The initial responses are likely to range widely. Some will indicate minimal loss due to manual back-up procedures and high loss. However, once managers begin to come forward with subjective statements like, 'I believe it is high risk', then the next step is to ask them to indicate more clearly what they mean by this statement. This then leads into the final request, which is to quantify the impact. At this point, a range of quantified expressions will exist on security risk levels.

3.2.3   STEP THREE: OBTAINING CONSENSUS ON RISK LEVELS

This is an essential step in obtaining the commitment by top management to the level of risk defined. A meeting should be arranged of the appropriate senior managers at which will be tabled the expressions of risk as defined. The purpose of the meeting will be to reach consensus on the risk levels, normally as a range rather than an absolute figure.

> A large insurance company with an integrated on-line system identified its life policy application as being high risk. During the preliminary interviews with its senior managers, there was a wide expression of risk, ranging from low at the one extreme to corporate 'death' at the other. Ultimately, the main impact of protracted suspension in processing was identified as the inability to collect premiums from its policyholders. Even then, absolute consensus could not be reached on the quantum of loss. After a meeting amongst the senior managers, consensus was reached that the loss would amount to between £7,500,000 and £10 million per month.

It will be seen from the above that the expression of risk in this manner permits the cost of security measures to be justified in an objective way.

3.3   Evaluating Security Measures

At this preliminary stage of reviewing computer security, it is not possible to come up with all of the detailed recommendations. These will only be arrived at once the full review of computer security described in the ensuing chapters of this book have been completed. However, it is possible to define the broad strategy to be adopted to meet the risk levels defined. This strategy will embrace:

1. Specified applications, programs and files.
2. The approach to prevention of abuse or disaster, detection plans.
3. Priorities, i.e. action which is needed in the short term and items which will need to be considered in further detail in the medium to long term.

3.4   Cost of Justifying Security Measures

The preceding steps lead naturally to the collection and presentation of all of the information needed for an informed decision on the costs and benefits of the computer security strategy. The information collected and decisions taken should all have been progressively documented and this can now be consolidated in a final report to top management. It is important to arrange a meeting of the top management concerned to review these findings and recommendations and obtain a decision thereon and approval of an action plan for more detailed investigation and implementation. The policy thus constitutes a framework for the approach which will be accepted and the cost levels which may be incurred without repetitive requests to top management.

4.   OBTAINING COMMITMENT TO THE SECURITY POLICY

At various stages during this chapter, reference has been made to the need to consult and involve top management. Top management will ultimately have the final decision on the approach to be adopted and on expenditure levels. Unless they have been involved in the preceding stages, it is unlikely that they will be fully committed to any decisions which may be taken. This lack of commitment will only be identified some time after many of the recommendations have been implemented at a detailed level.

Traditionally, the first problem is to establish who has overall responsibility for computer security. Most line managers look to DP management, while DP management have difficulty in accepting responsibility for security in user departments. There are two policy areas which need to be clarified:

1. Commercial risk issues.
2. Technical computer risk issues.

Commercial risk issues will ultimately be found to be the responsibility of line management. In the final analysis, it is difficult for them to abdicate responsibility for this. Technical issues will clearly be the responsibility of the data processing management. The division of responsibility in this way is practical but co-ordination is important to ensure effective meshing between commercial and technical functions. In large organisations the need for this co-ordination will ultimately rest in a very senior line manager. This person will rarely be someone who is not a member of the executive committee. In Chapter 12 we discuss the establishment of a computer security committee which would, *inter alia*:

a. *Agree the assignment of responsibility.*
b. *Participate in the definition of the security policy.*
c. *Monitor progress generally with the detailed implementation of remedial measures.*
d. *Periodically review and test the adequacy of computer security.*

The establishment of such a committee at the very early stage, when computer security policy is first reviewed and defined, is generally helpful. It ensures that appropriate members of management are involved from the start and consequently leads to a higher level of subsequent commitment.

5. SUMMARY

There is no 100 per cent secure system and in the final analysis, there is a high dependence upon the integrity of the people in an organisation. The implementation of meaningful computer security requires:

- The classification of an installation in terms of high, medium or low risk.
- The identification of high risk applications and within these programs and files which constitute high risk.
- The quantification of risk, preferably in financial terms.
- The evaluation of alternative strategies to computer security and the selection of the one which appears to be the most appropriate to the organisation.
- The cost justification of the selected strategy to top management.
- An approach leading to solid commitment.

Gaining the commitment of top management to the security policy is essential. This is best achieved by the involvement of all concerned in the preliminary work needed to define the security policy. The establishment of a security committee at this time is generally helpful and leads to more routine monitoring and high commitment levels.

CHAPTER 3

Organisation and Division of Responsibility

There are four aspects to the way in which computer activities are organised, which will have an impact upon computer security:

- Division of responsibility.
- Systems of internal control.
- Responsibility for security.
- Succession to key personnel.

Each of these is discussed separately.

1. DIVISION OF RESPONSIBILITY

In any organisation checks and balances on the quality of work are created by dividing responsibilities. For example, in a commercial concern control is enhanced by precluding those receiving cash from customers from having access to detailed customer accounting records and from initiating entries to them. Such a person is thus prevented from creating unauthorised entries and misappropriating cash. A number of examples exist in the context of the computer which reinforce the quality of management control and hence security.

1. Data preparation staff should not have access to operations activities.
2. System analysts and programmers should not have access to operations activities and vice versa.
3. Operators should not have unrestricted access to the librarian function or the department where master files are stored.
4. Operators should not maintain the only controls over work processing and should be barred from initiating error corrections.

A wide range of activities exist which should be organised to incorporate work divisions of the type outlined. Work division needs to be reinforced by sharp physical and procedural restrictions. The key elements of this philosophy are clearly defined functions which are self-contained. In the context of computer activities these key functions are:

- Systems development.
- Programming.
- Program maintenance

18

- Software support.
- Data preparation.
- Central and remote operations.
- Control.
- Librarian.

Separate divisions of work will also need to be incorporated in user procedures. These traditionally receive attention at an application level. (The relevant principles are discussed in Chapter 8.) Within the computer department there is often strong resistance to the implementation of effective division of responsibility on the grounds that the procedures inhibit flexibility and detract from general efficiency. Minimum security measures will reduce work flexibility but with careful design, efficiency should not be impaired. In most cases the personnel affected are not consulted when designing work divisions. They are consequently not committed to them and can be strongly demotivated. This in itself will create a situation which increases security risk which can easily be avoided with forethought.

The two key elements which serve to support many of the underlying divisions of responsibility are the control and librarian functions. These should preferably have a high level of independence, reporting to the highest possible authority, preferably the data processing manager. In some installations the control function is narrow, being concerned solely with processing controls. In others it is broad in scope and may embrace the librarian function as well as the responsibility for monitoring other activities such as systems, programming and operations documentation, key handover points from different functions and maintainence to existing systems.

The degree of division between the different functions will depend upon the level of security demanded in the installation. The overriding consideration is the independence of the control function and the staffing of this activity with personnel of the calibre commensurate with the skill demands which they will experience. Appendix 2 contains a part check-list with examples of key questions to consider in assessing the division of responsiblity and work in a computer installation.

2.   SYSTEMS OF INTERNAL CONTROL

Division of responsibility and systems of internal check combine to form the system of internal control in an organisation. The systems of internal check may be defined as:

The evidential checks which ensure that there is the complete and accurate collection of data and that the divisions of responsibility and authority referred to in the previous section are adhered to.

Typical documented evidential checks demand that:

1. Program amendments are adequately authorised and tested.
2. New systems are adequately documented progressively through development work and tested prior to handover for live production work.
3. File data in the form of new records or amendments thereto are adequately documented and checked by initiating departments against computer edit print-outs.
4. Input data is adequately batched and checked against data accepted for processing.
5. Errors are documented and error corrections adquately authorised and checked against computer print-outs.

The examples submitted are but a few of the typical evidential checks which exist within an organisation. Internal and external auditors have the responsibility for:

a. Reviewing the division of responsibility and procedures to ensure that they are sound.
b. Test checking to ensure compliance of the predetermined procedures or systems of internal check.

(Further reference to this responsibility is made in Chapter 10.) It is not the purpose of this book to provide a comprehensive check-list of these items. Reference, however, has been made to them in order to highlight the importance of these elements within the framework of the Total Security Concept. Numerous versions of comprehensive check-lists have been published by the various auditing and accounting authorities, but Appendix 3 contains an extract of part of a questionnaire to assess evidential checks in a typical computer system.

3.   ASSIGNING RESPONSIBILITY FOR SECURITY

The need for this has been discussed in the preceding chapter. It is important to specify this responsibility in the job descriptions of both commercial and computer management. If a management by objectives (MBO) philosophy is in use in the organisation, security should constitute one of the key result or performance areas. At the top management level, responsibilities will be of a policy nature. Examples at this level are:

1. Defining a security policy.
2. Ensuring the existence of disaster plans.

At progressively lower levels of management, the responsibilities will become increasingly operational and detailed. For example, the systems manager's responsibilities for security will include:

a. Identifying security demands in long range application plans.
b. Routinely implementing security measures in application design and implementation.

In a survey of over thirty organisations up to 1976, only two had security responsibility incorporated in any job descriptions. This is thus clearly a weak area in most organisations.

4. SUCCESSION TO KEY PERSONNEL

In the introduction to this book the dependence on key individuals was highlighted. An essential element in computer security is to ensure that all *key* personnel have adequate succession. In practice, it is not possible to ensure succession for *all* personnel so that the definition of key personnel needs to be carefully restricted. Particular caution should be exercised in evaluating the importance of personnel associated with advanced applications or systems software.

An argument which is frequently encountered when advocating succession is that of cost. Many installations are justified on the basis of inadequate staffing. As a result, cost levels do not provide for succession. If the installation is one demanding high level security measures, then expenditure levels must provide for adequate succession and back-up of key positions. If these cannot be afforded, then an organisation should carefully consider whether in-house computerisation is the appropriate way to process the required information. Other possibilities should then be explored, such as greater use of a computer bureau.

5. SUMMARY

The systems of internal control in an organisation are an important ingredient in computer security. The main elements of this are division of responsibility and systems of internal check.

It is important to separate certain functions. In particular the control and librarian functions should be clearly defined and independent of any operational functions. All procedures should incorporate systematic evidential checks in order to enhance controls.

Defining the responsibility for computer security is generally a weak area. Line management must assume overall commercial responsibility; technical responsibility should be clearly delegated.

The succession of key personnel is essential and budgeted expenditure levels need to incorporate provision for this, particularly in high risk applications.

CHAPTER 4

Physical and Fire Security

The importance of physical and fire security has long been recognised; these are areas which traditionally receive attention. However, while there is an apparent level of effectiveness, real protection is generally inadequate.

A number of separate areas are addressed in this chapter:

- Location and construction of the computer facility.
- Air-conditioning.
- Power supply.
- Flood risk.
- Access.
- Fire protection, detection and fighting.
- Housekeeping.

Each of these is now discussed.

1. LOCATION AND CONSTRUCTION OF THE COMPUTER FACILITY

1.1 Location

Past tradition has dictated that the acquisition of a computer installation should be publicised as much as possible. Accordingly, many computer installations were accommodated in glamorous glasshoused facilities with a maximum of publicity. These installations were generally sited on main roads with high pedestrian and motor traffic.

The threats posed to computer installations have rapidly changed this position. The siting of computer installations has become increasingly clandestine. Site selection has also become more conservative, with computers being located away from high traffic areas either surface or airborne. Yet many sites are selected in a short-sighted fashion.

> A large insurance company went to extensive trouble in planning its new computer facility. A monolithic concrete external shell was constructed and a multitude of security innovations incorporated in the design for access control. The site was adjacent to a large sub-economic housing area which for three months after the opening of the computer centre was the scene of extensive civil unrest.

22

1.2 Construction

Even after almost a generation of computer use, computer management have learnt little about the design requirements for high security installations. Conversely, architects are rarely well-versed in the design principles for high security computer installations. This is probably the major reason for the poor design of many high security computer installations.

The construction of the interior of the computer facility is also of essential importance. Traditional partitioning is rarely of adequate security. Many ceiling tiles, while rated inflammable, are combustible, and fireproof partitioning is inadequate for areas such as the computer library.

Glass creates a problem in the computer facility wherever it is installed as the accommodated activities can be identified or scrutinised. Thus glass should be avoided on all perimeter walls. Glass in reception areas should be reinforced, bulletproof and fireproof.

1.3 Layout

Considerable experience has been accumulated in the effective layout of computer facilities. The primary objective is usually efficient workflow, with security being of a secondary consideration. The data reception and distribution area is a high risk one most susceptible to external attack. It should, as far as possible, be isolated from the high risk constituents of the installation, such as data capture and processing. This requirement generally conflicts with workflow efficiency but is mandatory in high security installations.

Where the facility is located on a site which also accommodates other elements of the organisation's activity, extreme care must be taken in the positioning of this facility.

The computer installation at a medium-sized manufacturing organisation was sited at the end of a large factory. In all respects, the siting was adequate. However, the external wall of the computer room itself was the dividing wall with the factory. The other side, within the factory, was used as a corridor for fork-lift trucks carrying heavy loads. An accident on the external wall, which was constructed from normal partitioning, would have destroyed the wall and seriously damaged the computer on the other side of it.

2. AIR-CONDITIONING

Every installation experiences extensive difficulty with air-conditioning. The risk through air-conditioning is twofold:

1. The air-conditioning is essential to the environment in which the computer operates; major fluctuations or deteriorations can result in the need for the computer to be switched off.

2. Air-conditioning installations are a frequent source of fire and a substantial threat from physical attack, particularly through inlet ducting.

In order to address these risks, the following requirements should be met:

a. Back-up air-conditioning plants should be installed where high risk applications have been implemented.
b. Protective grids should be installed over all inlet and outlet ducting.
c. Fire shutters and detectors should be installed in ducts.
d. Effective audible monitors and alarms should be installed.

A major difficulty which is experienced with air-conditioning, particularly in warmer countries, is dust and external solar gain. Air intakes should not be at ground level and should be sited away from dusty areas. Careful consideration should be given to solar gain in the siting and construction of computer activities. This is another argument against glass windows, but where these are unavoidable, external blinds should be erected.

3. POWER SUPPLY

The power supply to air-conditioning, the computer and data capture equipment is important. In high risk installations, particularly those with on-line and real-time processing, back-up supply is essential. This back-up supply might also be necessary for network and terminal systems. It is impossible to back-up all aspects of a network but careful consideration must be given to key elements of it.

Continuity of power supply is not the only issue. Stability is the most important consideration, In areas adjacent to industrial sites or large office complexes, surges in power supply are a frequent phenomenon. Such surges can damage stored data, programs, or the equipment, and regulating equipment should be installed where these problems arise frequently.

4. FLOOD RISK

In many parts of the world, flood damage and risk is commonplace. The risk to computers is substantial. In these areas, computers should not be sited in basements or ground floor areas but preferably high up in a multi-storey structure. This might create other security problems but these can be effectively countered. Obviously the best approach is not to site the computer in areas where flood risk is a reality.

Flood or water damage has occurred even where installations are not located near rivers or low-lying areas. This has arisen from burst pipes or blocked drains. The location of pipes in the construction of the computer facility is thus an important consideration. Damage from blocked drains is a material risk where the computer is located in a basement area. Water or flood detectors should be installed if this is the case, as should emergency pumps, to deal with unforeseen flooding.

A large building society located its installation in the basement. An undetected blockage in the sewerage pipes caused an overflow of the sewage over the weekend. Sewage flooded down the stairs into the basement where the computer was located. Six inches of sewage was found in the basement on Monday morning when the staff returned to work.

It can thus be seen that damage and inconvenience can be caused by elements not directly related to an installation.

5.   ACCESS
The following principles require evaluation in designing the access procedures for a computer installation.

5.1   Controls over Access During Different Times of the Day or Night
Controls over access will vary during different times of the day. It is important to ensure that procedures are as rigid at night as during the day. In particular the controls during tea-breaks and shift changes are important.

5.2   Access by Third Parties
This embraces air-conditioning and computer engineers, visitors — and cleaners! These and all other third party personnel need to be:

1. Security cleared with adequate identification.
2. Controlled and monitored in their activities during access.

An old ladies club was taken on a tour of the computer installation. On the conclusion one of them took a postcard out of her handbag which she had removed from a tray *en route* and asked the guide if he could read it for her. It was never discovered where the card had actually come from.

Third party maintenance and other personnel should be identified in advance of arrival on site. The risk from these personnel is as great as any other visitor.

5.3   Structure and Layout of the Reception Area
This risk is paramount, especially in high security areas where the possibility of physical attack also needs to be considered. Employees or visitors should be identified and admitted one at a time. In high security installations, automatic magnetic and other searches may also be incorporated in this reception area. If it is necessary to use glass in the construction of this area, reinforced glass should be used.

In most high security installations, there are often two or three *'layers'* of physical security to protect access to the reception area. The first level of protection is a high visibility security fence around the perimeter. This often lulls an organisation into a false sense of security, especially as most staff working inside have been security cleared. Inferior control is applied to access within the perimeter exposing the high risk installation to unnecessary danger.

5.4   Burglar Alarms and Proofing

All areas should be secured against physical intrusion. Burglar alarms, proofing and steel sheeting should be used, as far as possible, in a circumspect fashion so that undue attention is not attracted to the fact that there is a high security facility. Such measures should apply not only to the computer room and/or to the facility but also to any perimeter areas. The construction of doors and windows should receive particular attention in order that they are secure.

5.5   Card-Keys and Badges

These are currently a highly popular form of access control. Badges integrated with card-key systems do, however, have an enhanced value. However, *'tail-gating'* or following someone through a door which is held open, is commonplace in virtually every installation. Certain electronic systems are now on offer which provide enhanced forms of control yet they will not be totally effective unlesss human disciplines are maintained.

While much can be done to bring physical access standards up to a high level of security, it will be seen that like everything else, it can never be 100 per cent secure. Physical access will thus need to be reinforced and supported by other elements of security. Dependence on it alone will be foolhardy.

6.   FIRE DETECTION

Considerable experience now exists in fire detection methods and apparatus. It is, therefore, not proposed to describe these in complete detail. A number of salient elements need to be observed:

1. Fire and smoke detectors need to be carefully sited in relation to air-conditioning, as this may diffuse heat or smoke through airflow, thereby preventing the detector from being activated.

   A large high security installation installed a very costly comprehensive detection system. It was overlooked that the air-conditioning design was such that a pool of air was continually blown across the ceiling of the computer room. A fire would only be detected once it had already reached significant proportions.

2. The smoke detector selected should detect different kinds of smoke. Certain detectors do not detect the smoke or fumes from burning plastic which is used as insulation in electrical wiring, and consequently fires caused by short circuits may not be detected.
3. Smoke and heat detectors need to be located in the computer room, adjacent office areas and perimeter physical locations.
4. Smoke and heat detectors need to be located under the floor and in air-conditioning ducting.
5. Fire alarms should be connected to the central alarm at the site, or directly to the fire department.

7. FIRE PROTECTION

The requirements for fire protection in the physical construction of the facility have already been noted. As with detection, it is important that these requirements are not only incorporated in the construction of the computer room itself but also in adjacent areas, e.g. stationery stores.

Special storage facilities will be needed for magnetic tapes and discs which are held on site or at remote points. Considerable experience has been developed by the manufacturers of the safes for storage purposes. However, care should be taken to ensure that any facilities which are procured meet the minimum standards laid down by the Fire Insurance Association and other standards institutes.

A large computer user spent over £25,000 in acquiring some new safes. Three years later, during a routine security review the fire classification of the safes was questioned. The safes had been manufactured in a foreign country and the labels had to be interpreted. It was found that they were sub-standard.

Fire protection also needs to be provided for systems, programming and operations documentation. The destruction of this documentation can preclude the use of back-up programs or files. In many high security installations this has either been overlooked or the documentation on hand is out of date. Procedures need to be established for ensuring that all documentation is kept up to date on a routine basis and that security copies are stored in a remote location with security copies of files and programs.

A large on-line installation was destroyed by fire. Back-up programs, master files and operating instructions were available and operations were restarted within a day or two. All the key systems and programming documentation was destroyed. It took over six calendar months and many man-years of effort to recreate essential documentation. In the interim there was great disruption every time a fault occurred in processing.

8.   FIRE FIGHTING

Considerable experience also exists in this area and it is thus proposed to only highlight common deficiencies.

Gas dousing is commonplace in most computer installations. General use is being made of carbon dioxide, often hesitantly, because of its lethal effect on personnel. In recent times other gasses have been placed on the market which are effective as extinguishers but do not have the same lethal effect on personnel. The use of gas for dousing is currently a source of considerable controversy due to the acidic effect of all gasses at high temperatures. It is likely that this will be an area of continuing change.

Gas dousing can be of dubious value in installations sited in multi-storey structures. However, the effectiveness of this form of extinguisher is high when the fire starts in the computer room. Careful consideration thus needs to be given to fighting fires which do not start in the computer room.

Appropriate extinguishers should be sited within ready access. These extinguishers and the gas-dousing equipment should be regularly tested in order to ensure that they are operating effectively.

Fire-drill procedures should be defined and documented and all staff should be trained in their use. This is typically found to be an area weakness especially in installations with high staff turnover rates. Many personnel are frequently unclear as to the action they should take in the event of a fire.

The involvement of the fire department in designing and implementing fire detection, prevention and fighting procedures can be invaluable. Many fire brigades, however, still fight fires on a traditional basis and they will need to be carefully briefed on their actions. In several instances, firemen have been seriously injured when an axe has been used to break into a computer room filled with carbon dioxide gas. The fire department should be briefed on the procedures to be followed in fighting fires in areas adjacent to, above or below the computer room. Extreme damage can be caused to the computer equipment by fires in these adjacent areas.

Respiratory equipment should be to hand both in the computer area and for use by the fire department in the event of a fire. Burning magnetic tapes give off noxious fumes and fires of this type need to be fought with respiratory equipment.

9.   HOUSEKEEPING

The cleanliness of a computer installation is important from two points of view:

1. It reflects a disciplined attitude. Security is very much an attitude of mind and this reflects that the right and effective procedures are in use.
2. Poor housekeeping creates the scope for breaches in security, i.e. doors or

windows not closing properly or scope for fire, e.g. waste paper or boxes stored in corners of rooms.

Good housekeeping reflects the general attitude of the people in an installation. It represents good management and enhances computer security.

10. SUMMARY

Physical and fire security is the area of traditional focus when assessing computer security. However, there are still many deficiencies even in high security installations.

Key areas for review are:

- The location and construction of the computer facility.
- The location of air conditioning, the existence of back-up and effective monitoring of air-conditioning performance.
- The stability of and existence of back-up power supply.
- Flood damage risk through storms and breakages in parts.
- Physical access especially with regard to third parties, i.e. non-employees and structure.
- Fire detection, protection and fighting procedures.
- Good housekeeping which reflects a positive attitude of mind to high level management and security.

Physical security in its own right will not ensure a secure installation. It needs to be viewed in conjunction with the other elements incorporated in the Total Security Concept.

CHAPTER 5

Personnel Practices

Most organisations realising their increasing dependence upon the integrity, stability and loyalty of personnel, are devoting more attention to this area of computer security. The employment of sub-standard staff in positions of high responsibility, e.g. operations and control, is not uncommon and must increase risk from accident.

As has already been stressed, there is a risk that excessive dependence can be placed upon this area, especially in high security installations where it is routine practice to obtain security clearances for personnel. These installations are always a target for attack and any person intent on this would ensure an immaculate security clearance.

Five areas are reviewed in this chapter:

- Recruitment practices.
- Performance appraisal procedures.
- Leave policy.
- Job rotation.
- Personnel attitudes.

1. RECRUITMENT PRACTICES

Virtually every organisation has a well-structured and routine recruitment procedure. However, in many, this is laxly applied. Important features in recruitment practices from a security point of view are:

- Reference checking and security clearances.
- Psychological testing.
- Medical examinations.

1.1 REFERENCE CHECKING AND SECURITY CLEARANCE

It is commonplace to undertake reference checking. However, for legal and other reasons, many organisations are reluctant to provide meaningful references. This presents major difficulties in evaluating the acceptability of an applicant employee.

Even where the referee is willing to provide information, the past employer often provides information of such a generalised nature that it is difficult to get a specific feel for the integrity of the applicant. It is highly desirable that a detailed check-list be compiled for use in this regard. Standard personnel check-lists are generally adequate for this purpose and many versions are available in published form. These checks can rarely be too thorough.

A recruitment agency was retained to find a data processing manager for an organisation. Generalised and written reference checks were procured as part of the recruitment service. One of the senior managers in the company was dubious of the integrity of the applicant. He made his own enquiries and found that the applicant was an alcoholic.

Insurance companies can also assist with the reference-checking process. The need for fidelity guarantee cover is referred to Chapter 9. Where this cover is required, the insurance company will undertake its own independent checking. This reinforces the reference-checking procedure.

In a high security installation, it is routine to obtain police security clearances. While these are generally most vigorous, even they cannot be a 100 per cent correct.

1.2   Psychological Testing

The use of psychological testing during the recruitment stage is an important potential reinforcement. This testing is not only suitable for evaluating aptitudes, but also for assessing attitudes, social values, political feeling and general stability. In many high security installations these tests have been found to have increasing value. Highly professional services now exist and they reinforce the other procedures referred to above.

A large insurance company became aware of major deficiencies in its recruitment procedure. As a result, a psychologist was retained to aptitude test all existing staff. These tests identified several staff holding key positions who represented security risks to the organisation.

1.3   Medical Examinations

An important part of recruitment procedure are medical examinations. These assess not only the physical fitness of an individual but can also be used to evaluate the attitude and potential stability of the new recruit. In particular, ability to deal with stress should be analysed, especially where this will be one of the job demands.

Some organisations have introduced the practice of six-monthly or annual medical examinations for computer staff in high stress jobs. If adverse elements are detected, an individual's job may be temporarily restructured.

2.   PERFORMANCE APPRAISAL PROCEDURES

Performance appraisal activities can routinely enhance security. While they are primarily directed at measuring managerial or work effectiveness, these can enhance security effectiveness. Simultaneously, the appraisal can be used to assess work attitudes and general feelings towards the organisation. While it is in no way suggested that managers become amateur psychologists, personnel with personal and attitudinal problems can be identified and helped through the appraisal process.

> A large computer user expanded the questions in its six-monthly performance appraisal to incorporate some check-points on attitude and motivation. As a result, the chief programmer was found to have personal problems with his marriage, health difficulties and obviously not in a position to assume stress. His job responsibilities were redistributed for a six-month period to help him over his difficult time.

In high security installations, it is merit-worthy to have each manager review the attitude and behaviour of his personnel at more frequent intervals, say quarterly. A four-to-six question check-list can easily be compiled for this purpose.

3.   LEAVE POLICY
Excessive overtime is commonplace in data processing installations. At the same time, leave is rarely enforced due to the key positions held by personnel.

The enforcement of leave is important to ensure that personnel in stress positions are adequately rested periodically. Computer personnel are generally of above-average qualification and intelligence, frequently highly-strung, and while no statistics are available, the incidence of nervous breakdown has been noted. Employers thus show inadequate responsibility by not enforcing leave.

In all other departments of an organisation, leave is regularly enforced, particularly in positions of trust. This is an important way of detecting theft, fraud and potentially planned sabotage. The importance and dependence upon key skilled personnel should not preclude the enforcement of this practice in the data processing function.

4.   JOB ROTATION
Job rotation is generally known as a sensible counter to fraud, especially where personnel are in a high position of trust. This principle should also be applied to computer personnel.

It should be noted that there is a disadvantage to job rotation, especially in a high security environment. This is that an individual can be exposed to activities across a broad front. However, job rotation is generally most practical at middle and junior levels where the situation does not arise. Even then, the advantages of job rotation generally far outweigh any potential disadvantages.

5. PERSONNEL ATTITUDE EVALUATION

A well-motivated employee is unlikely to be disloyal. Conversely, the scope for breaches of security due to accident or deliberate attack is higher in an environment where motivation is poor. In many installations, particularly the larger ones, it is difficult to keep track of attitudes at all times. The use of attitude surveys can be a valuable tool for routinely monitoring this aspect of personnel policy.

6. SUMMARY

Personnel practices are an important element of computer security. However, overdependence on them is common, especially in high security installations.

A number of factors need to be considered as part of the personnel practices, mainly recruitment, performance appraisal procedures, leave, job rotation and general attitudes. Most of these aspects are routinely reviewed outside the DP function, but irregularly within data processing.

CHAPTER 6

Insurance

1. TRADITIONAL PROBLEMS

Commercially, the insurance industry is long-established, with well-defined philosophies and disciplines. But any organisation seeking advice and guidance on the insurance of its computer risks generally experiences considerable difficulties. There are two major problems:

1. There is a major communications gap: insurance advisers generally know a lot about general commercial risks but little about computers, while computer personnel know a little about insurance and a lot about computers.
2. Risk-exposure and consequence is frequently not clearly understood due to the youth of the computer profession and the relatively limited history with insurance claims.

The impact of the foregoing is that few computer users have all material risks adequately covered. The tendency is to latch on to one or two obvious areas such as hardware replacement or fire cover. Less obvious areas such as the cost of recapturing data or the extent of consequential loss are generally skirted.

Certain of these difficulties probably flow from general problems with insurance. Few organisations routinely review the risks and the cover which are required. Policies are frequently found to be out of date. Experience with some fifty computer installations has revealed that in not one instance were all of the material risks adequately insured.

This is certainly worse than the normal commercial situation. It is difficult to pinpoint the exact cause, but the communications gap referred to above would appear to be the major one. Many experienced insurance service organisations are unable to get to grip with detailed computer issues for this reason. In some respects they are discouraged by jargon and attitude of computer personnel who are more concerned with the technical elegance of their computer installations and less with the tedium of a commercial issue such as insurance.

In this chapter we review:

- The insurable risk areas.
- Specialised insurance services.
- Changing risk exposure.

2. INSURANCE RISK AREAS

There is very little comprehensive published material on computer insurance risks. However, the National Computing Centre (NCC) has published an excellent booklet, 'Computer Guide 7: Insuring a Computer System'. This summarises the key insurable risk areas extremely well.

2.1 Environment

Environmental risks arise from either external sources or from conditions within the computer system/facilities.

External risks emanate from sources in close proximity to any computer facility. They may be inherent in the nature of the business or they may be adjacent:

1. Explosives and flammable materials or processes.
2. Toxic, heated, gaseous, dusty or abrasive atmospheres.
3. Flood risk in low-lying areas.

Internal risks emanate from malfunctions of the services upon which the computer depends:

a. Power supplies.
b. Air-conditioning equipment.
c. Fire, heat and smoke detectors, carbon dioxide or gas-dousing and water-sprinkling apparatus.
d. Water-containing apparatus, e.g. central heating, sewerage.

There are other risks such as breaches of security or safety procedures, and unauthorised access which may cause damage or subsequent business interruptions.

All of these risks can usually be covered by conventional policies.

2.2 Equipment

Equipment embraces the total computer installation, i.e. the building, furniture, air-conditioning plant, ancillary equipment, power suppliers, tape, cards, stationery, etc, and the computer itself. The latter will include any centralised processing equipment, terminal systems and networks. An insurance policy which is arranged for the computer itself may not be appropriate for some of the items in the installation, and it may be necessary to have more than one policy. The first essential step, however, must be to obtain adequate cover for the computer itself. The other items can then be considered.

2.2.1 RESPONSIBILITY FOR INSURANCE

In any installation there is a mixture of leased and purchased equipment.

Leased or rented equipment needs to be considered separately as the agreement with the vendor generally has specific provisions. In many instances, the vendor has his own insurance cover and further insurance would amount to duplication. However, generally speaking, all such cover excludes insurance of negligence by the installation's own staff and this will need specific consideration.

Accordingly, the relevant contracts need to be examined and, where appropriate, the suppliers contacted to obtain clarification on their cover and the risks to which they are exposed.

Certain risks such as negligence will be difficult to insure. The possible consequences of negligence should have been examined as part of the Total Security Concept and minimum standards, procedures and disaster plans defined. The fact that these embrace non-insurable areas should be carefully assessed in implementation planning.

Purchased equipment or facilities will require insurance. It is important that in all instances these resources be insured at replacement value rather than at cost. Most insurance policies now incorporate 'Average Clauses', in terms of which the insured will be paid out at an averaged down figure if the insured cost is lower than replacement price. Replacement costs should thus be reviewed frequently in order to ensure that they are up to date.

2.2.2   RISKS TO BE COVERED

The most common approach is the use of an 'All Risks' type of policy which embraces both the external and internal causes of damage. This may also include business interruption cover which is reviewed below. The main risks to be covered are:

a. Damage from external causes. The prime external peril is fire, but certain special perils, e.g. lightning, may need to be considered. Occasionally, special perils can be added to the organisation's standard fire policy, e.g. earthquakes, flood, burst pipes, impact damage, riot, civil commotion, etc. The main point is to ensure that all of these have been considered.
b. Damage from internal causes. Many of these items are not insurable. However, examples of typical risks include:
   - Deliberate or negligent actions by operators which result in damage to the equipment.
   - Damage resulting from a prolonged stoppage of the air-conditioning plant.

These risks require specialist advice as they can frequently be covered as part of the organisation's Loss of Profits or All Risks policy.

2.3 Software and Data

2.3.1 DEFINITIONS

The word *software* needs to be specifically defined in the context of the particular organisation. It should certainly embrace:

a. Operating systems, utility programs, etc., usually supplied by the computer manufacturer.
b. Application programs obtained from third parties.
c. Programs which have been developed in-house.
d. Operational programs belonging to third parties which are in the care of user (usually covered by some contractual arrangement).

The word *data* is intended to cover such items as master and transaction files and data held in its source state.

2.3.2 INSURANCE AGAINST LOSS OR DAMAGE

The terms software and data are not generally referred to as such in many insurance policies. They are more likely to be referred to as business records. Care should thus be taken to ensure that there is a correct understanding between insured and insurer as to the range of media being covered. In particular, it is common to find that the storage media, e.g. disks or magnetic tapes, have been insured for their purchase cost, but that the data stored thereon is not adequately insured. Accordingly, computer system records should be insured for:

a. Loss or damage to the media.
b. The cost of reinstatement of the records thereon.

A careful analysis needs to be conducted of the replacement and reinstatement costs to ensure that all relevant factors have been fully considered.

2.3.3 SOFTWARE

The type of protection mentioned previously only covers loss or damage following the occurrence of an insured peril to the computer and associated software. This is probably satisfactory for operational risks but there may be others which cannot be covered by a material damage type policy. For example, software could be:

a. Taken out of the building and lost.
b. Stolen.
c. At other premises which were damaged.
d. Inadvertently or deliberately damaged by a third party.

In these circumstances, software could be regarded as an object rather than as a part of a system, and it may be necessary to insure it in that way. The determination of the value that is to be covered would need to be agreed with the insurer. The value should be arrived at by considering:

a. The costs of creating the hardware.
b. The costs of recreating the software.
c. The commercial value of the software.

In addition, removal or destruction of the software as described above may have a consequential value giving rise to delay or business interruption. Provision needs to be made for this risk as well.

2.4   Business Interruption and Recovery

Damage to a computer results in a reduction in its 'value'. The function of material damage policies is to restore the value by providing funds for repairs or replacement. Such damage may also give rise to inability to perform certain operations and this could have a financial consequence for the business. These risks should be covered by a business interruption or loss of profits policy, in order to provide financial compensation for any consequential loss or increased costs of working.

2.4.1   ASSESSMENT OF THE CONSEQUENCES

The construction of hypothetical considerations should not be considered as restricted to damage of the computer itself, but also to related areas such as ancillary equipment and communication systems. The subject is extremely complex as it may embrace:

a. Standing charges which remain constant even though the business is operating at a reduced level of activity.
b. Additional costs of working to minimise the effects of loss in earnings.
c. Depreciation in the value of perishable items.
d. Penalties for late delivery.
e. Disruption in control systems which may result in imbalanced production or stock levels.
f. An inability to invoice or to collect outstanding debts.
g. Delays in implementation of new systems which could delay the production of new goods or services.
h. General administrative disorganisation with repercussions on the trading areas of the company.

It is usually possible to cover many of the above areas through normal contingency plans. However, each of the material risks should be identified, contingency plans reviewed and the required level of insurance risk determined.

2.4.2 COST EFFECTS OF INTERRUPTION

Having identified the risks, a full financial analysis should be completed of the alternative courses of defensive action and the likely costs of each. Two elements should be specifically incorporated in such insurance cover:

a. Increased cost of working only.
b. Loss of profits or revenue.

2.5 Personnel

The risk situation which can stem from action, attitudes or circumstances involving personnel are not new and are generally covered by existing policies. They are briefly summarised in this section in order to highlight the elements for review and the incorporation in existing policies.

2.5.1 DAMAGE CAUSED BY PERSONNEL

Damage can be accidental, malicious or negligent. Resources and software should be specifically covered for these types of damage.

2.5.2 INJURY TO PERSONNEL

There are several additional potential injury risk situations:

a. Electrical or mechanical risks.
b. Risks emanating from protective devices such as CO_2 extinguishers.
c. Risks resulting from exceptional working conditions.
d. Risks from lack of knowledge of computer or non-computer personnel.

To cover and minimise these risks, employers and public liability policies should be reviewed.

2.5.3 DISHONEST ACTIONS BY PERSONNEL

Key computer personnel should be covered by the organisation's fidelity guarantee policy. As referred to in Chapter 5 dealing with personnel practices, this step serves independently to reference check employees for any dishonest record in their work histories.

2.6 Third Party Liabilities

Computer equipment may be used by third parties and this creates additional risks.

The contractual position between the organisation and third parties should be carefully reviewed and documented. Consequential loss to third parties should be excluded in such contractual arrangements, or else specifically limited. Consequential loss insurance cover is for all practical purposes unavailable.

3. SPECIALISED INSURANCE SERVICES

Certain organisations now offer specialised services for computer users. These include the provision of staff who have deep knowledge of computer working and consequently of the risks involved. In addition, several international insurance companies have now developed specialised policies for insurance users.

The use of specialised organisations or organisations offering these areas expertise is most helpful in evaluating insurance risk and policies. It contributes significantly to bridging the communication gap referred to at the outset of this chapter.

4. MONITORING CHANGING RISKS

Insurance risks are changing progressively, both within the organisation as a whole and within its computer activities. It is important to ensure that new risks are covered and the policies are kept up to date.

A valuable approach is to establish a computer insurance committee. This would work as a sub-committee of a security committee referred to in Chapter 11. The purpose of the committee would be:

1. To identify and quantify direct and consequential risks flowing from the organisation's computer installation.
2. To ensure that cover is reviewed to take account of escalating costs or replacement prices.
3. To ensure that adequate contingency plans exist especially where insurance cover is not obtainable.
4. To ensure that consequential loss is excluded from the organisation's liability to third parties.
5. To obtain specialist advice and guidance where this is required.

The committee should comprise representatives of the following:

a. Data processing management.
b. Insurance company.
c. Insurance brokers.
d. Secretarial or financial control department.
e. Internal or external audit.

By arranging regular meetings from quarterly to annually, depending upon the size of the installation, it is possible to ensure that risk coverage is clearly identified and kept up to date.

5. SUMMARY

The communications gap between computer personnel and insurance specialists is a major problem in arriving at adequate insurance cover. Computer insurance risk areas embrace:

- The environment in which the organisation or the computer installation is sited.
- Hardware.
- Software and data.
- Business interruption.
- Personnel.

Specialised services are available from certain insurance and broking organisations. These include the provision of staff and/or tailored policies.

An insurance committee should be established comprising representatives of all affected parties to ensure that insurance risks are regularly reviewed and to improve communications.

PART 2
TECHNICAL AND PROCEDURAL ELEMENTS

SYSTEMS SECURITY
APPLICATION SECURITY
SYSTEMS PROGRAMMING AND OPERATIONS STANDARDS
THE ROLE OF INTERNAL AND EXTERNAL AUDITORS
DISASTER RECOVERY PLANNING AND TESTING

CHAPTER 7

Systems Security

1. SCOPE OF THE TERM

Systems security is primarily concerned with the security of the computer equipment and embraces:

- Hardware.
- Generalised software, i.e. excluding specific application programs.
- Networks, i.e. data communication lines and systems.
- Terminals and directly related generalised software.

Each of these is now discussed in turn. The main area to be addressed in each instance is the weaknesses or 'trapdoors' which expose the system to threat or abuse by a person with specialist systems knowledge.

2. HARDWARE

Generally, hardware trapdoors are only of significance in high security installations. In such installations, it is necessary to identify all of the trapdoors and to determine how they can be kept secured. In many instances, this is best achieved with physical catches or covers.

Apart from the specialised needs of high security installations, there are general risks which apply to all installations. A good example is the switch which exists on a number of tape decks by means of which parity checking can be evaded. These switches should be removed or suitably secured. Depending on the suppliers of equipment, other similar trapdoors may exist which should be closed.

Finally, there are malpractices in hardware operation which create risks through negligence or accident. These should all be defined and incorporated in a standard practice manual for operations personnel. Where practicable, these practices should be monitored through the equipment, by surprise test or observation.

3. SOFTWARE

The scope for software trapdoors is considerable if not infinite. A completely secure operating system has not yet been devised. A team of experts in the United States at the Lawrence Livermore Laboratories is under contract to the Department of Defence to specifically test and identify the weaknesses in operating systems. This team has not yet found a completely secure system.

45

A key finding which has emerged from their studies is that few, if any, operating systems have been designed with security as a primary objective. Security is generally considered as an afterthought and, as a consequence, the measures which are introduced are frequently superimposed on an existing design structure. This naturally detracts from the level of effectiveness in security.

Software trapdoors represent a substantial and fundamental threat to system security. Much of the software today is highly sophisticated and there are only a few people with knowledge of all the intricacies incorporated in the design. Consequently, the knowledge needed to counter abuse only rests with a few personnel. Concurrent with this situation, software aids have been developed which in themselves represent security threats. A good example of this is retrieval or interrogation software, which can provide unauthorised information on program or file structures, or access to private information held on files.

Typically, software security is aimed at:

1. Restricting access to programs and files.
2. Ensuring that operators can operate without detailed supervision and not modify programs or files.
3. Ensuring that the right data, files and programs are being used for processing.

In general, significant developments have taken place to enhance security in all of the three areas. However, many trapdoors still exist. It is important to identify and define each one of these. This is a lengthy and extensive exercise which can only be undertaken by personnel with detailed knowledge of the systems in question. The approach is to:

a. Compile an inventory of identified trapdoors.
b. Compile an inventory of trapdoors which have not yet been identified but which are postulated.
c. Test existing and potential trapdoors to validate their existence.
d. Define any form of monitoring or off-setting controls in each area of weakness.
e. Compile an action plan for the implementation of such off-setting controls.

It is essential to involve key staff from the relevant suppliers in this activity in order to contribute independence to the exercise. The general level of trapdoor knowledge within supplier organisations is small and it may be necessary to retain an independent consultant to assist with this evaluation. For obvious reasons, the amount of published literature by both suppliers and others in this area is virtually non-existent.

4. NETWORKS

This term is intended to describe the data communication systems and associated management software. Like software, this is also an extremely complicated area with a small body of specialists who have knowledge of it. The major threat is unauthorised access to the network with a view either to gaining confidential information or making unauthorised use of processing facilities. Published cases of abuse in both of these areas exist. The best known is the Pacific Telephone Case where a computer specialist gained access to a network-operating manual and, using this and his own terminal, used the company's data processing facilities to defraud it of stock and run his own business.

In the extremely high security installations, careful consideration should be given to gaining access to confidential data. As in the case of a telephone line, it is not difficult to tap a data transmission line. The only real measure of security is to make use of coding or cryptography in order to preserve the confidentiality or privacy of data, even when a breach of security is committed. Good *scrambling* equipment for cryptography is also available.

5. TERMINALS

Many terminals today represent powerful computers in their own right, making use of sophisticated software. Accordingly, a review of terminal security should treat terminals as small computer systems. The principles for reviewing hardware and software outlined above should thus be applied.

The key issue to terminal security is unauthorised use. The following factors need to be reviewed:

1. The location of terminals, general knowledge of this, and physical access to the terminal itself.
2. Control over unauthorised operation of the terminal by physical keys, codes or other identification methods.
3. The hardware, software and other checks to ensure that the controls referred to above are enforced.

While the network and mainframe software for controlling terminals has been substantially enhanced in recent times, a completely foolproof terminal security system has not yet been identified. As a result, it is important to ensure the maximum off-setting controls in the following areas:

a. Physical checks and reports of terminal use.
b. Monitoring and reports on unauthorised access attempts.
c. Surprise changes of user codes.
d. Surprise and unknown audit tests which are conducted as a concurrent part of the data processing.
e. Surprise tests of operating practices.

6. PERFORMANCE MONITORING

An essential part of systems security is a detailed analysis of systems performance. There is a danger that one can become concerned with the more obscure and complex abuses and the obvious ones, such as unauthorised jobs or use of time, are ignored.

> A large computer user was experiencing regular and intermittent faults with its computer time clock. For some reason or another, these could not be rectified. After a while it was just accepted as a flaw of the computer and no more attempts were made to fix it. It was subsequently found that the Operations Manager and one of the supplier staff members were in collusion with one another and that excess time was being used to run an illegal service bureau.

Some suppliers of equipment offer comprehensive monitoring software, others do not. There is also a wide range of independent hardware and software monitors available, some of them at low cost. These all facilitate use analyses and effectiveness measurement and will highlight unplanned or unauthorised processing.

Controls which should be introduced as part of the system of internal control are:

1. Spot comparisons between actual and planned job runs, and particularly the files and programs of which are used.
2. Software for monitoring rejections by the operating system of the terminals and users to specified files or programs.

7. SUMMARY

Systems security is a highly technical and complex part of computer security. A methodical approach is required for identifying trapdoors, defining off-setting controls and ensuring that these are implemented and observed. This review should embrace mainframe hardware and software, networks and terminal hardware and software.

Monitoring mainframe, network and terminal performance is an important management and security function. The facilities offered by existing software or enhancements thereto should be carefully considered. In addition, the scope for monitoring attempted penetration of programs or files should be monitored and reported on.

CHAPTER 8

Application Security

1. SCOPE

The term 'application security' embraces the computer and non-computer components of each application. On the computer side it embraces the data, files and programs, as they are processed within the system. The non-computer elements embrace the collection and submission of data and master-file information for processing, controlling this information to ensure that it has been correctly processed and redistribution gets to the user. The classical stages of each system embrace:

1. Manual initiation of data.
2. Conversion of data into computer acceptable format, i.e. data capture.
3. Computer processing.
4. Distribution of output.

2. THE COMMON FLAW: THE CONNECTION BETWEEN THE COMPUTER AND THE USER

In many installations, careful consideration is given to the controls in both the user and computer departments. However, because different people are evaluating the controls in each area, gaps frequently arise at the interface or connections between the two areas. A good example of this is modifications to standing data on master files. An unauthorised change to a credit limit is initiated. It is difficult for data preparation or computer personnel to validate the authority of the master-file amendment which is accepted for processing either separately or together with other credit data. Some form of control over this type of record is thus necessary. This is typically achieved with sequence checks on documents and value controls on batches as well as manual checks conducted against computer listings by the user. At the same time, checks can be made of the authorisation of the various documents.

Routine controls in these areas have been commonplace for some time and now generally effective. Weaknesses only arise when discipline is not sufficiently rigorous. There is merit in manual spot-checks against master-file print-outs in order to check the possibility of master-file errors or unauthorised changes.

A major problem area in every computer system is the control over errors. A number of key points exist:

1. All errors must be corrected.
2. The errors should only be corrected by authorised personnel.
3. Division of responsibility must be carefully maintained in assigning the authority for error correction.

In practice, all of these issues generally present practical difficulties. A highly rigorous and methodical approach is needed.

Another important point at the man-machine interface is the distribution of data. Considerable care and security may be exercised over input data fed to the computer and equal care can be exercised over processing within the computer department. However, little care may be exercised in distributing reports to users.

A large computer user produced highly confidential sales analyses which showed profit contribution, market share and other competitive data. Considerable care was exercised in the processing of this data and the reports were carefully wrapped on completion for transmission for users. Low-level clerical staff were used to collect the information. A clerk could not resist the temptation when sent to collect the reports and key information was photo-copied. The reports were re-wrapped and submitted to the user. It was only by accident that the organisation learnt of the sale of the data to a major competitor.

Security insofar as distribution needs to embrace the following:

1. Responsibility and identification of personnel authorised to access of the reports.
2. Control over output for both valid and aborted runs.
3. Control over the one-time carbons from decollated reports.

The competitor of a large international firm was extremely amused to learn competitive information from computer print-outs which his child brought home from nursery school. The reports were from an aborted run and the reverse side had been used for drawing paper at school.

3. USER CONTROLS

The user has the primary responsibility to ensure that the data which is collected for processing is complete and accurate. He must also ensure that all of this data has been processed and is incorporated in the reports which are returned to him. In the final analysis, it will not help the user to blame the computer for decisions on inaccurate data.

The manager of a large brewery was sacked when he took a decision to produce more draught beer than was required, based on an erroneous computer report. The surplus draught had to be poured down the drain.

It is insufficient for the user to pass responsibility for these controls to the computer department. He cannot abdicate this responsibility. Whilst the creation and maintenance of these controls does represent some duplication, they would be required with any other type of system, i.e. quasi-manual methods incorporating accounting machines. These controls to ensure correct transaction and master-file data are an integral part of the system of internal check in an organisation.

4. COMPUTER PROCESSING CONTROLS AND FILE SECURITY

4.1 Computer Processing Controls

These represent the controls maintained within the computer department. They are a mirror of the controls maintained by user departments, but in some respects they are more detailed, e.g. detailed run-to-run controls between programs.

The controls within the computer department are procedural and arithmetic. The procedural controls include:

1. Division of responsibility between data capture and operations.
2. Division of responsibility between operations and the library.
3. Evidential records reflecting the transfer of records and data between the different functions.
4. Control over the accuracy and distribution of output.

The prime purpose of these controls is to ensure the complete and accurate processing of data and files using the correct programs. The arithmetic controls are to ensure the complete and accurate processing of all data records both during and at the end of processing.

4.2 File Security

A major and traditional element of focus in processing control is that of file security which should embrace the following:

4.2.1 SECURITY COPIES STORED AT A REMOTE LOCATION

The location for the storage of these files should preferably be some good distance away from the computer site. In very high security installations, special measures are often taken.

Traditional procedures rarely take account of the security measures in force while transporting discs or tapes from the computer site to a remote location and vice-versa. In high security installations this represents a real risk area. Accordingly, the activities should not be performed by one individual on his own.

An operator with a grievance deliberately corrupted magnetic tapes with a magnet as he unloaded the security copies from the tape drive. He had planned to irreparably damage the installation over a period of time. Fortunately, an unexpected call for security copies identified that they were corrupted and exposed his actions.

4.2.2   FILE IDENTIFICATION AND CONTROL

This embraces physical checks of hard copy labels and physical records for the movement of such files, as well as the file-header identification checks which are performed routinely by software.

In some instances this is deficient and modifications should be incorporated to remedy any weaknesses.

4.2.3   FILE ACCURACY

The installation standards should incorporate in programs detailed run-to-run controls and record counts. Detailed balancing of record by record and/or binary counts should be incorporated. The checking and reconciliation of these arithmetical counts should be balanced against the manual run-to-run controls maintained by the control function.

4.2.4   PHYSICAL ACCESS TO FILES

In many installations there is unrestricted access to the tape library. In other cases, access is restricted but protection is poor. The tape library represents a great concentration of data and files and there is considerable scope for risk or abuse.

Computer operators should not have routine access to the tape library which should be controlled by separate individuals who preferably report to someone other than in the operations function. The discipline of making available data and files against production runs is a difficult one, particularly insofar as scheduling for unplanned work. However, many installations have made appropriate arrangements and now deal with this problem routinely.

5.   REGULAR APPLICATION CONTROLS REVIEW

The review of computer and non-computer controls in an installation is an important part of the function of internal audit. (This is dealt with separately in Chapter 10.) Such a review is a complex and demanding task requiring extensive time. It is not uncommon to find that three to four months is required for large and complicated applications. This type of work is not a routinely accepted function in many installations, even in high risk ones. The practice is, however, increasing. There will be a considerable amount of start-up work initially and, depending on the size of the audit team, it is not unusual to find the duration of initial work to be of the order of twelve to eighteen months. Thereafter, however, the routine activity will involve less workload.

6. SUMMARY

The scope of application data and file security embraces both computer and non-computer work. Careful consideration needs to be given to the interface between the computer and non-computer activities. User controls cannot be abdicated to the computer function. The controls maintained in the computer centre are generally of a very detailed level, particularly with reference to files and programs.

The on-going review of application controls is an important part of the internal audit function.

CHAPTER 9

Systems Programming and Operations Standards

A number of problems arise in incorporating the whole area of standards as part of any security programme. The biggest and most basic one stems from the fact that standards and documentation are generally not perceived as being related to the issue of computer security. Flowing from this is the often-quoted traditional argument that the additional effort required for effective security is disproportionately high and that management must choose between operational effectiveness and computer security.

In reality, virtually no incremental effort is required where good standards, practices and documentation have been implemented within a computer department. This, then, reinforces the view that where you have above-average management, above-average security is a logical consequence. As mentioned previously, sound standards of practices, and particularly the use of structural techniques, automatically enhance security for applications which are in the course of development, are being maintained, or have already been completed and are operational. Security issues do need consideration during various quality assurance check points, but then these ought to be considered automatically.

It will be seen from the foregoing that the real issue then is not a security one, but one of commitment to good work standards. This is still an issue facing many computer departments. It stems from the evolution of the industry, with its technological bias, rather than an emphasis on sound management practices. With the effluxion of time, emphasis is moving, and in the last decade with increasing momentum, towards machine independence and management practices as opposed to technical issues. As a result, new trainees are receiving a fairly comprehensive introduction into effective standards when they enter the profession.

A medium-size computer user, with a central processing facility and a number of distributed locations, decided to review computer security. At that stage, while documentation was recognised as an important part of security procedures, the process of progressive quality assurance during development was reviewed and determined as being unrelated to the issue of computer security. At that time, the standards and documentation systems, programming and operations work were of a mediocre quality. Five years later the company reviewed its work practices and enhanced these significantly. The improvements included the implementation of structured techniques for systems analysis, design and programming. Simultaneously, a report was conducted criticising the company's poor restart capabilities on many large systems, and the inability to implement advanced computer auditing techniques. An analysis revealed that extensive effort and cost would be involved in rewriting the company's systems to bring them up to a minimum acceptable standard.

As a result of these findings, security issues were comprehensively reviewed and incorporated in the company's new standards. With the benefit of hindsight, the company had learned that security was very much a part of its work practices. Unfortunately, it had not been perceived at the first review; the company subsequently spent over $500,000 rectifying basic security defects in its operational systems.

This is frequently the area, too, which causes the most reaction to any formal review of computer security. The most typical question is, what have these standards to do with security?

A large organisation with a centralised processing facility and distributed minis decided that a complete review of computer security was necessary. A check-list was compiled of the areas for review. This embraced all of the areas incorporated in the total computer security concept. However, systems and programming standards were omitted.

The systems and programming manager reacted strenuously to any suggestion that this area be incorporated in the security review. Even after repeated explanations, he indicated very clearly that he was not prepared to incorporate this into the security review. As a result, these standards were omitted from the audit. A few months later, the systems and programming manager resigned from the company. A separate review was conducted of the security aspects of systems and programming standards. Major security gaps were found.

As will be discussed in this chapter, there are two major reasons for reviewing standards as part of computer security:

1. The need to consider security during the preliminary and all of the detailed stages of analysis and design.
2. The demand for adequate back-up arrangements, including duplicates of systems, programming and operations documentation.

The consideration of standards is divided into two parts: systems and programming, and operations.

1. SYSTEMS AND PROGRAMMING STANDARDS
Security, in turn, needs to be considered at two levels:

- For the installation as a whole.
- Specific applications.

The consideration of security requirements for the whole installation requires long-term planning in order to ensure that security is catered for with the implementation of progressive applications. There is thus a long-term connotation which can clearly be seen in any installation where a decision is taken to enhance application security. Major revisions are generally required to applications and a long time-frame is involved. On the other hand, consideration of security in individual applications has a shorter-term connotation.

1.1   Long Term: Security and Computer Planning
Computer security is rarely stated as a primary design objective. As a result, many applications are already designed and implemented when security is first considered. The omission of security features at this stage in applications will usually require costly major revisions.

Clearly, this approach is unacceptable with the increasing complexity, scale and level of investment of applications. In the complex on-line, real-time and data base applications which many organisations are currently implementing, material if not major re-design effort can be involved to incorporate minimum security standards. It is therefore important to incorporate security objectives and standards as an integral part of the long-range computer planning activity. Key features to be considered are:

1. The impact of computer security on hardware and software strategy.
2. Terminal security considerations with regard to:
   a. Application controls.
   b. Physical requirements and location.
   c. Network strategy, security and back-up.
3. Application control standards, particularly restart and back-up standards.
4. Data and file design standards.
5. Internal and external audit role and requirements during the design, implementation and operation phases.

The level of experience in computer planning as a whole is generally relatively low due to the relative youth of the computer industry. Consequently, only a minority of installations have a well-structured and clearly defined approach. This is a key prerequisite to the incorporation of security standards in the planning phase. Security aspects require routine consideration at each check-point in the planning process. While there are unique items to consider from a planning point of view, many of the items to be reviewed can be clearly identified by listing the security elements which should be routinely reviewed in implemented applications.

1.2 Short Term: Application Quality Assurance

Within this framework of the computer plan, individual applications will be designed and implemented. Average applications involve a typical timeframe of three to six months, while more complex on-line ones could require up to two years of elapsed time to implementation. Within each application, a number of aspects require routine monitoring at a detailed level. Ideally these should be incorporated as check-points within the system and programming standards and documentation. The major elements for review are:

- Software and hardware security.
- Application controls.
- Work methods and supervision.
- Documentation.

1.2.1   SOFTWARE AND HARDWARE SECURITY

The application security requirements will vary according to the type of application and the security levels demanded by the organisation or its computer installation as a whole. Generally speaking, these issues will have been addressed during the long-range planning. However, it is possible that installation demands for security as a whole may be low, but some highly confidential application is being implemented.

During the initiation phases of the project, security objectives should be clearly defined. These should embrace consideration of transaction data, master-file standing data and program security. If terminals are used, the issue of terminal access will require careful consideration. Clear definition of these aspects will permit the formulation of clear design criteria and strategies.

1.2.2   APPLICATION CONTROLS

Few, if any, installations have escaped the dilemma of omitted key controls from applications. Controls like security are rarely a primary objective, with the consequence that major revisions are generally required in order to incorporate them. Control needs fall into two categories:

a. User controls.
b. Detailed run-to-run data and file controls maintained by operations.

In a well-established installation, it is unlikely that major new control standards will arise. The minimum standards have already evolved through bitter experience.

An organisation invested £250,000 in designing a large on-line order entry application embracing invoicing, stock control, debtors accounting and credit control. Security and control requirements were considered at the early stages of the project, but many were omitted on the basis that the new design philosophies incorporated in on-line processing made many traditional controls old-fashioned. As a result, many essential record counts, file controls and audit trails were not provided for.

Extreme difficulties were experienced in implementing the application and it was soon found that errors could not be pin-pointed without the normal essential controls. Many major revisions were required to file and program designs to incorporate them. The ultimate cost of the additional effort was nearly £100,000.

Apart from the routine controls referred to above, a major consideration, and one which is assuming increasing importance with larger applications, is that of restart philosophy. This tends to be another 'poor relation'. While much generalised and operating systems software facilitates restarts, this will always be difficult unless specific provision has been made for it in the application design. Accordingly, restart philosophy needs to be a stated design objective right at the start of the project and successively detailed consideration needs to be given to it at suite level and within individual programs.

1.2.3   WORK METHODS AND SUPERVISION

It is generally true that security is good where there is effective management. This can be extended to situations where there are well-structured and defined standards for work method. Structured methods incorporating regular check-points and reviews also facilitate supervision. While even the closest supervision will not necessarily detect fraudulent or unauthorised routines in systems and programs, it can certainly deter abuse. But more importantly, it will ensure that security standards are routinely considered during the design process. Major security considerations as part of the design process are:

a. Clearly defined handover points; these reinforce division of responsibility and enhance quality control.
b. Testing and conversion programs; the implementation of new applications is a risk-prone period and highly structured and controlled steps are required.

Both of these areas are typically weak. Convenience and time-pressures generally erode the disciplines of handover, while few installations have structured and well-defined standards for the planning and execution of tests for individual programs and overall suites. This is particularly true in the case of on-line systems where terminals require new and enhanced testing standards. All of these aspects need to be carefully incorporated in the security standards.

Another important security consideration is the potential loss of investment in systems which are in the course of development.

The project leader of a large application was reviewing a material part of the design concepts. He left the documentation in the back of his car. This was stolen and the documents were never recovered. Nearly fifteen man-years of effort were lost.

This experience is not unique. Documentation should be progressively copied and stored in a secure place during the course of development. Similar risks also apply where large files are in the course of being converted, particularly when the source data is in existing manual records.

The introduction of the new range of techniques to improve programmer productivity, such as structured design and programming and the programmer team concept, considerably enhance security. The formal structuring of work modules and detailed quality evaluation by several staff members provides a rigorous framework for security and a basis for evolutionary documentation or documentation which is progressively completed. These practices should thus be encouraged.

1.2.4 DOCUMENTATION

Reference has already been made to the security considerations for projects in the course of development. Similar precautions are necessary for completed applications. The main ones are:

a. The storage at a remote location of the documentation for all applications; maintenance modifications will need to be routinely incorporated.
b. Access to documentation should be restricted to personnel who are directly involved with the project and in high security installations perhaps only to modules of that application.

Most experienced DP personnel recognise that back-up copies of files and programs are only of use if supported by adequate systems and programming documentation. Yet few installations have meaningful procedures for the routine protection of this. Even where these do exist, access is generally unrestricted and any member of staff can legitimately remove, study or copy applications documentation. These practices destroy the benefits of division of responsibility and facilitates deliberate abuse in the form of theft, fraud or sabotage.

The data processing manager of a small installation was concerned about the risk of fire to his installation. This was housed in a new building which was inadequately protected against fire. Many of the applications had only recently been developed or were in the course of going live. Due to lack of support from top management, he took the precaution of copying all source-decks and documentation and keeping these at home. A fire gutted a major part of a new building, including his computer installation. His premonition and diligence were rewarded. It was only then that management responded to his request for enhanced security.

2. OPERATIONS

Like systems and programming documentation, an installation can be put at considerable risk through the absence of:

1. Adequate standards for operations activities, including, where relevant, data preparation.
2. Storage arrangement for duplicate documentation.

In most installations, there is acceptance of the need for systems and programming standards. This is not generally true of operations standards, although the minimum of operating instructions is generally accepted.

Operating standards should incorporate:

a. Good housekeeping practices.
b. Hardware and software operating malpractices to be avoided.
c. Procedures when using security copies of programs, data or files.
d. Handover procedures for new applications.
e. Stages in mounting new applications.

These requirements apply equally to data capture facilities where they form part of the operation function. Generally speaking, the standards are less complex although the increasing introduction of remote and on-line data entry is changing this situation.

As in the case of systems and programming documentation, application operating instructions need to be duplicated and installed at a remote location.

3. SUMMARY

Systems, programming and operating standards and documentation have an important impact on computer security. Security requirements need to be routinely reviewed as part of the long-term computer planning process, as well as individual application development and implementation.

The existence of effective work methods will enhance security and provide adequate documentation by way of by-product. Careful consideration needs to be given to access to this documentation in order to reinforce decision of responsibility. Back-up copies of all documentation should be stored at a remote location.

CHAPTER 10

The Role of Internal and External Auditors

Surprise is often expressed about the fact that the audit function constitutes a part of the Total Security Concept. Care has been taken so far to demonstrate that each element of the concept is important, both as free-standing and when integrated within the concept. The aim of this chapter is to demonstrate that the audit function is a most important element.

It is not the purpose of this book to present a treatise on computer auditing. Accordingly, while the scope and roles of internal and external auditors are summarised and the important aspects of computer auditing and their impact on computer security are carefully highlighted, a detailed exposition is not presented of computer auditing techniques.

1. GENERAL AUDIT ROLES
1.1 External Auditors
The external auditor's responsibilities are primarily of a statutory nature. In most countries his responsibilities are clearly defined by statute. Generally, the key legislation is a Companies Act or the equivalent. There are, however, a wide range of other statutory areas which require the involvement of a registered auditor, e.g. banking or insurance legislation.

Sometimes the external auditor will, by agreement, undertake special work. However, this rarely detracts from the auditor's primary function to express an opinion on accounts produced by an organisation based upon an examination of the books and records. Hence, contrary to common belief, the auditor is not responsible for the detection of fraud.

1.2 Internal Auditors
The internal auditor has no statutory responsibilities. His scope of activities will vary from one organisation to another. In some cases he has a high-level role which aims at reporting on the managerial effectiveness of the organisation; in others his role is primarily to check on systems and procedures and to see that these are being enforced.

Accordingly, the role of the internal auditor, which has been an evolving one over the past fifty to seventy-five years, is not an extension of that of the external auditor. Instead, the internal auditor is very much a part of the systems of internal control within an organisation. This is how the internal auditor's function has evolved — a form of internal inspector.

It is usual to find that the internal auditor's scope of activities is narrow rather than broad. However, the current trend is towards a much broader role, with the internal auditor undertaking management and operational audits. In this context, the internal auditor is also becoming more involved in computerisation. Among many large computer users, where there has been increasing sophistication of applications, the need for greater involvement by the internal audit function has been recognised. Thus, the internal auditor's activities will typically embrace:

1. Active involvement in the develoment process, ensuring that adequate audit and security requirements are incorporated, and also participating in reviews at project check-points.
2. Review of application systems and controls in both user departments and at computer processing centres.
3. Reviewing computer security policy and procedures and actively participating in disaster tests.
4. Introducing advanced techniques for the auditing of sophisticated computer systems.

In line with this practice, the reporting relationship of the internal auditor has been elevated, and in many cases he now reports to the chairman of the board or chief executive officer.

It will thus be seen that the internal auditor has a vastly different scope of responsibility to that of the external auditor. The only real impact which the one has upon the other is that the work undertaken by the internal auditor may relieve the external auditor from considerable detailed work, due to his enhancing the system of internal control in his organisation.

2. COMPUTER AUDIT ROLES AND SECURITY

It will be seen from the foregoing summary that both internal and external auditors constitute an important independent check upon the effectiveness and hence security of computer activities. Internal control and security are generally more effective in well-run organisations. The existence of an independent check and report-back on the effectiveness of computerisation is thus of value. Security can be enhanced by bringing specific focus to bear on the procedures in force for the prevention of breaches of security, the detection thereof and recovery procedures in the event of some disaster.

A number of important issues need to be addressed in ensuring an effective contribution from the audit function to computer security:

- Scope of internal audit in computer security.
- Clear liaison between internal and external auditors.
- Role of internal audit in society.
- Role of internal audit in operational systems.
- Education and training for effective internal auditing.

2.1   Scope of Internal Audit in Computer Security

In the previous section, reference was made to the differing roles of internal audit in various corporations. In the case of computers, few auditors have the deep technical knowledge to participate extensively in auditing through rather than around the computer. A 'communication gap' typically exists in that auditors rarely have any deep computer expertise, while few computer personnel have any deep audit exposure. In many cases, this results in auditors being actively discouraged from auditing through complex computer systems, programming or operations activities. This will substantially diminish the contribution which the internal audit function can make to computer security.

2.2   Liaison between Internal and External Auditors

A clear case has already been made for close liaison between the two parties. This can result in a major reduction in the work undertaken by external auditors. However, many new techniques such as integrated test files, concurrent processing, audit 'hooks', etc., require extensive on-site time. The application of these techniques is accordingly generally the domain of the internal auditor. He can, however, draw on specialist advice from the external auditor who, from his exposure to many organisations, can contribute extensive technical expertise and concentrated experience.

The internal and external auditors should therefore carefully define the required demands from an audit point of view, and the roles and approaches which they will adopt to meet these. Carrying through the principles to application will result in a detailed set of questionnaires for reviewing internal control and for confirming that systems and procedures are working as they should. Guide-lines will be compiled for the application of the specialised audit techniques referred to, including generalised audit software for comparing and stratifying files, extracting statistical samplings and reports. The resultant enhanced effectiveness must improve computer security.

2.3   Role of Internal Audit in Development

In most systems, security cannot be made effective unless detailed controls and recovery procedures are incorporated in initial design. Few existing systems have had security as a prime objective. As a result, considerable sums of money have been expended in incorporating security requirements in systems which are already operational.

The internal auditor has an important function in participating in long-range applications planning, and detailed application design and implementation, in order to ensure that audit and security needs are addressed from the outset. At the same time he can bring an independent approach to bear at the various project milestones. With the increasing number of advanced and large-scale systems, these contributions increase the reliability of the system's development progress and avoid unnecessary expenditure subsequently.

2.4   Role in Operational Systems

The internal auditor has an important role in bridging the gap between user and computer centre controls. With adequate training, he can conduct detailed controls reviews in the user and follow through data into the computer processing itself. This role is most important in avoiding abuse of operational applications.

No system is static and the organisational demands are changing all the time. As a result, operational systems are subject to on-going and repetitive modifications. An independent assessment of computer controls over the whole spectrum of the application is thus important on a routine basis.

This is certainly a major responsibility area of the internal auditor, and his objectives and approach should be carefully structured in addressing it.

Finally, the organisation and procedures in the computer function will have a major impact upon the effectiveness and security of computer applications. It is, therefore, important that the internal auditor should be adequately trained to review this area.

2.5   Education and Training

Much has been said over the past ten years about the need for training in computers. However, when one really gets down to assessing the amount of effective training work that has been done, it is clear that the results achieved are only limited. Most training has a technical focus and very little emphasis is placed on machine-independent functions. The main training need is in the application of proven management methods to the new area of the computer in general and computer security in particular.

This is also the case with the audit function. Audit practices and procedures have existed for a considerable time. What is needed is an understanding of the technical issues so that the established principles can be properly applied. Certain new technical areas such as data base, on-line and real-time systems do create new differences. However, the principles remain unchanged; it is the application which varies.

One of the biggest problems in ensuring that the audit function makes a realistic contribution to computer security is the provision of adequately trained personnel. It has been difficult for some time to obtain staff adequately trained in audit procedures. Add to this the need for computer skills and the position is compounded. A further factor is that there has been very limited training available for either auditors or managers in the objectives, scope and approach of computer auditing and, in particular, management's approach to computer security.

There are a number of distinct areas which need to be addressed in training auditors and management for an effective contribution to computer security:

1. Application controls objectives, security measures and recovery procedures.
2. The responsibility for internal control.
3. The role and scope of internal audit.
4. Specialised control needs in advanced applications — training for systems analysts and designers and auditors.
5. Advanced audit methods for auditors.

Few of these can be obtained from computer suppliers or management institutes. However, a few of the accounting societies now offer courses and most of the large international firms of public accountants have established training courses which are offered to their clients.

3. SUMMARY

Internal and external audit functions play an important role in computer security. The major items for consideration are:

• The scope of internal and external audit.
• Liaison between internal and external audits.
• The roles of internal audit in the development and operational stages of systems.

Agreement has existed for a long time on the need for internal audit to participate extensively in computer systems and security. In practice, few organisations can reflect much achievement. Probably the biggest difficulty in this regard is obtaining real commitment from line management, computer personnel and auditors to implement the procedures which have been summarised in this chapter. The introduction of effective training will do much to facilitate this.

CHAPTER 11

Disaster Recovery Planning and Testing

The remarkable fact is that most companies perceive that they have adequate disaster recovery plans which would meet most caegories of disaster. The reality is that most of these plans are shallow, unstructured and inadequate in the face of the pressures flowing from an actual disaster.

During the past ten years, I have advised over sixty international corporations in areas of computer security and, specifically, in disaster recovery planning and testing. Of these, only one passed its first disaster recovery test. Most of the companies required three disaster recovery tests before any form of preparedness existed, and one large corporation made ten attempts before its disaster plans were proved to be anything close to adequate.

Many companies do conduct what they describe as disaster tests. These primarily take the form of running their work on a back-up machine. While this is certainly a component of any disaster plan, it is only a small one. There are a wide range of other issues, as outlined in this chapter.

Most companies resist disaster tests initially on the grounds of impossibility. This is especially true with on-line and real-time systems.

A financial institution with large on-line systems repeatedly argued against the practicability of any worthwhile disaster recovery test. The basis of the argument was that they could not contemplate the non-availability of their systems for an hour, not to mention a day or two.

After careful evaluation, it was found that a meaningful disaster could be conducted by setting up a parallel stream of processing operated on the basis that a disaster had occurred. This testing included a full test of the network, swiching facilities to back-up equipment, etc. This was a most complex exercise but, in reality, it closely simulated the possible impact of a real disaster. As a result of the successful outcome of at least two of these tests, management were persuaded that at some stage user preparedness had also to be tested. This was done by restricting the non-availability of computer processing capacity to specific branches and departments. The test highlighted a number of important gaps in the company's disaster plans and training programmes.

This experience has highlighted the findings of many corporations using an effective approach to disaster recovery testing. Not only does the simulated environment often create a combination of circumstances close to reality but the pressures generated highlight unthought-of possibilities or flaws in the plans themselves.

A very large computer user operating on data bases at a number of sites spread over a variety of geographic locations conducted a surprise disaster recovery test. At the time the test was conducted, security copies had been made of the largest data base. These were in the computer room awaiting transportation to the remote locations. They were 'destroyed' in the simulated disaster. The possibility of a disaster arising at that particular time had not been contemplated.

One of the major objections to disaster recovery tests is cost. This will, of course, vary according to the frequency with which the tests are conducted. Working on an average frequency of two to three times per annum for a large site, the costs are generally not material. Viewed in relation to the potential risks, especially in a high-security situation, the costs represent a low insurance premium for many items which are often not insurable. One of these may be corporate survival.

1. TYPES OF DISASTER
In considering disaster planning and testing, it is first necessary to delineate carefully the different types of disaster which could arise:

1. Complete destruction of centralised data processing facilities.
2. Partial destruction of centralised data processing facilities.
3. Destruction or malfunction of environmental resources for centralised data processing, e.g. air-conditioning, power, etc.
4. Total or partial destruction of decentralised data processing facilities.
5. Total or partial destruction of user manual procedures used for collecting input data to computer systems.
6. Loss of key computer personnel.
7. Disruption by strike.

Disaster planning procedures need to consider carefully the types of disasters outlined above. Specific plans need to be compiled for each eventuality. In each case, consideration also needs to be given to the likely cause of the disaster, i.e. accident or a deliberate attack. This will have a bearing on the recovery procedures which will need to be instituted.

2. SCOPE OF DISASTER PLANNING
Disaster planning needs to embrace applications in the course of development as well as operational applications. In the case of operational applications, there are a number of areas which need to be protected against disaster or resources available for recovery:

1. Systems, programming and operations documentation.

2. Processing facilities embracing:
  • Equipment of all types.
  • Environment for the equipment.
  • Data and files.
  • Programs and software.
  • Stationery.

The disaster-planning procedures will need to define in considerable detail the arrangements which have been provided for in each case, the organisation and responsibilities for implementing the arrangements and a step-by-step framework for initiating and implementing recovery procedures. These are now described in more detail in the next sections.

3. APPLICATIONS IN THE COURSE OF DEVELOPMENT

An analysis of computer projects reveals that they are growing in size, although today they are perhaps structured better, particularly with regard to modularity. As a result of this and the rising cost of systems and programming staff and equipment testing time, the cost of applications is increasing dramatically. A disaster could arise at an advanced stage and measures will need to be taken in order to ensure that the possible large investment has not been lost. Apart from the direct cost of lost systems and programming effort, there is potential loss to the corporation from delays to commercial operations in the implementation of computer services or information.

Theoretically, a disaster could strike at any stage of the development of an application. However, on the basis of Murphy's law, it usually tends to strike when the application is almost complete but documentation is not yet finalised.

It is important that a careful review be undertaken at each check-point or milestone of the project to ensure that there is adequate protection against disaster. While this may seem like over-reacting, the rewards can be significant should an accident happen. Accordingly, security and disaster considerations should be incorporated as standard questions in the review at the end of each completed phase of work.

It is well worthwhile bearing in mind that there will always be some costs incurred in the event of a disaster, no matter how good the disaster planning. Proving losses is always a laborious process and this is exacerbated in the absence of project-costing records which should also be safely stored.

4. COMPLETED APPLICATIONS

4.1 Systems and Programming

Previous chapters, and specifically Chapter 9 dealing with systems, programming and operations standards, referred to the need to store master copies of this documentation. This is undoubtedly a poor relation area. Applications are undergoing change all the time and in many cases documentation is not modified to reflect what is actually happening in practice.

A large motor manufacturer had implemented an on-line system for the management of his parts' inventories. The computer centre was destroyed by a freak fire. Security copies of data, files and programmes existed and good contingency plans had been implemented very quickly for the running of the application on back-up equipment. However, all systems, programming and operations documentation was destroyed for both applications in the course of development and those which had been completed. It took this organisation nearly twelve months to recover from this loss.

Disaster plans should thus not only provide for the existence of such documentation but for the eventuality which may arise should this documentation be lost.

4.2 Processing Operations

This embraces the whole system from the time that the required service is provided or report is produced. As a result, disaster planning must embrace user procedures and activities, if appropriate, transmission and network facilities, centralised processing, and the redistribution of output to user points. Disaster planning will need to be considered for each of the points as a separate entity and for the system as a whole.

4.2.1 EQUIPMENT

Disaster planning must cover equipment used at every stage of the system process:

- Terminals or data entry equipment.
- Processing equipment.
- Environmental equipment, i.e. air-conditioning, power.
- Distribution facilities and arrangements including network and terminals.
- Guillotines, bursters and decollators.

It is surprising how the destruction of a comparatively simple piece of equipment can constitute an important link in the chain of the system.

4.2.2 DATA AND FILES

Reference has already been made to the need for data and file security and back-up in Chapter 7. Disaster planning and recovery in this area is a detailed subject requiring very detailed planning. Each application will need to be carefully reviewed and the necessary arrangements made for data and files. A point that is frequently overlooked is that there are often considerable quantities of transaction data. As the recapturing of this data can involve large periods of time, the retention of transaction data in computer readable form is an important consideration.

4.2.3 STATIONERY

Continuous stationery often requires considerable lead-time from order to delivery. Emergency stocks of stationery need to be kept at some separate site in order to avoid difficulties in the event of the destruction of the main store of stationery. The stationery should embrace:

- Source data.
- Reports and output documentation, e.g. invoices, statements.

4.2.4 PROCEDURES FOR DISASTER

Written procedures will be required for each application. These will need to differentiate between the various types of disaster outlined earlier on in this chapter. The procedures should clearly specify:

a. Responsibilities in the event of a disaster, and the organisation which will become effective.
b. The immediate action to be taken:

- Organisation and responsibilities for resuscitation procedures.
- Classification of type of disaster.
- Establishing what has been destroyed.
- Determining priorities.
- Communication of situation to users and general management.
- Action plan for resuscitation.

c. The disaster plans should be specified in as much detail as possible. People tend to forget that when a disaster arises there is not the time to think about what do you do now. It is possible to anticipate the bulk of situations and these should be provided for in the disaster plan.
d. All staff need regular training in the disaster plan. The fact that there is high staff turnover in many data processing organisations is often overlooked.
e. The implementation of good practices which enhance security must be made routine, e.g. closing safes for magnetic data after the files or discs have been retrieved.

The disaster plans and documentation need to be communicated to a small group of personnel, but a sufficient number to ensure diversification. Excessive communication of disaster plans is also a security threat.

5. DISASTER TESTS

While many organisations have compiled disaster plans, few have attempted simulated tests of these plans. Disaster testing is important for the following reasons:

1. The awareness and preparedness of personnel for meeting disaster is tested.
2. Omissions in disaster plans can be identified.
3. The surprise nature of disaster tests is a good moral check to ensure that good security practices are being routinely enforced.

5.1 Scope of Disaster Tests

The tests will be one of the categories of disaster outlined earlier in this chapter, i.e. total or partial disaster. They should embrace user and computer procedures.

5.2 Timing of Disaster Tests

Disaster tests should be conducted sporadically. In the same way as cash counts and debtors' circularisations are initiated on a surprise basis, disaster tests should be unannounced. The planning of disaster tests will require that one or two people are aware of the test and this knowledge should be restricted, otherwise the surprise element will be lost.

Disaster tests do require experience and it is suggested that the first test be timed at a relatively convenient moment. However, actual disasters rarely arise at the most convenient time so that after one or two tests, the disaster test should be undertaken at a highly inconvenient time, i.e. when there is a heavy work-load. This is not going to be popular but it will be a very good test of the realism of the recovery procedures.

While realism is important, it is also necessary to recognise that there is a risk in disaster testing. Unless careful plans are compiled for the test itself, damage can be caused by the disaster test. One case is known of where the disaster test nearly turned into a real disaster!

5.3 Form of Disaster Test

The disaster test will take the form of a simulated disaster. An announcement will be made that a disaster of a particular type, e.g. fire or accident, has arisen, and all staff will be instructed to follow disaster procedures. The following should occur immediately:

1. All work should stop temporarily so that a note can be made of the status of processing.
2. An inventory should be compiled of any records which would have been destroyed as a result of the disaster.

Once this has been done, work can be recommenced although it is preferable periodically to take the test right through to use of back-up equipment and supplies, temporarily suspending all processing on the organisation's computer.

5.4   Analysis of Impact
The following inventory is compiled:

1. Application in development.
2. Operational applications either being processed or not being processed.
3. Records lost.
4. Report of staff responses and details of inadequate knowledge.
5. Quantification of loss due to destroyed records or disruptions in process.
6. The effectiveness of recovery and back-up procedures based on the use of actual back-up records and equipment.

After the completion of the above, a careful analysis should be compiled of weaknesses which were detected during the test. A detailed action plan should be compiled for the implementation of changes to ensure greater protection from a real disaster.

6.   SUMMARY
The real test of effective security is the responses which will be provided in the event of a real disaster. Effective response can only flow from effective disaster plans and well-trained staff who know what to do based upon the particular type of disaster. Good disaster planning should, therefore, embrace:

- Applications in the course of development.
- Completed applications.
- Procedures for different types of disaster.

The existence of disaster plans should be tested with surprise disaster tests. These disaster tests should be used to enhance and improve disaster plans.

PART 3
IMPLEMENTATION

IMPLEMENTING EFFECTIVE COMPUTER
  SECURITY
APPENDIXES

CHAPTER 12

Implementing Effective Computer Security

Little of the content of the preceding chapters will be of a revolutionary nature. Indeed, most of it is commonsense. It could be argued that the quality would be questionable if it were not.

As is the case in so many areas of endeavour, the principles are known. People know what to do but they rarely follow through and do them effectively. A key element to effective computer security is the successful implementation of the Total Security Concept. As a result, this is probably the most important part of the book. It describes:

- Defining the scope of computer security.
- Establishing a computer security committee.
- Confirming the scope of computer security within the organisation.
- Reviewing the current practice and effectiveness levels.
- Implementing security measures.
- Compiling an action plan.
- Disaster planning and testing.
- Monitoring the security demands of long range computer plans.

1.   DEFINING THE SCOPE OF COMPUTER SECURITY

Most organisations adopt a narrow approach to computer security. It is hoped that this book will have motivated the need for a broader one. This is a point of principle to be approved at an early stage. A policy commitment will be required by top corporate management as well as data processing management. Experience reveals that this can best be achieved by a half-to-one day workshop with pre-work, which embraces the following:

1. The increased pressures for computer security.
2. The need for a broader approach to computer security.
3. Discussion of each of the elements of the Total Security Concept.
4. Compiling an action plan.

This action plan ensures that all participants in the meeting will be clear as to what happens next. Typically, key action points are:

a. The establishment of a computer security committee.

b. Agreement on a security audit.

c. An action plan for defining security policy within the organisation.

The initiation of this, the initial phase of an effective approach to computer security, is usually the most difficult. Usually, someone in top management will have to be the motivator, otherwise matters continue 'as usual'. A valuable, albeit unfortunate, stimulus is some experience of computer abuse, either in the organisation or through a close associate.

2.   ESTABLISHING A COMPUTER SECURITY COMMITTEE

Probably the major reason for ineffective security is the lack of commitment by all concerned to what needs to be done. Everyone readily agrees with the principles, but few are committed to real implementation — and show it by real achievement. The only way to secure commitment is by involving all of those who are affected by computer security measures in the design and implementation of those measures. In this context, the use of a committee is highly appropriate, particularly bearing in mind the number of people who are likely to be affected.

2.1 Objectives

The main objectives may be summarised as follows:

1. Ensuring effective computer security within the organisation.
2. Designing and implementing effective disaster plans.
3. Reviewing security effectiveness levels using disaster tests.

A number of other objectives could be defined but these will be sub-sets of the main objectives outlined.

2.2 Constitution

Committees are difficult to manage at the best of times and the size should be limited. However, a number of different people will need to be involved:

- Top management.
- Data processing management.
- Security management.
- Internal and external audit.

At different stages, it may be necessary to involve others, insurance brokers for example.

2.3 Method of Operation

The primary purpose of the committee should be to co-ordinate activities rather than to assume any management responsibilities. In the first instance, the committee will co-ordinate the review of existing practice and the implementation of appropriate remedies. Thereafter, it will be responsible for on-going monitoring of practices through disaster tests and specific investigatory reviews.

One of the first tasks of the committee will be to construct an action plan for its activities. Dependent upon this action plan, the frequency of meetings is likely to be fortnightly to monthly at first. Once the bulk of the initial work has been completed, quarterly or even six-monthly may suffice.

The chairman of the committee should preferably be a representative of senior management, i.e. a member of the Executive Committee. This underlines the commitment of top management to computer security.

3.   REVIEW OF CURRENT SECURITY EFFECTIVENESS

Often, this work is undertaken by an external consultant. The rationale is that a high level of independence is necessary for this work and the comprehensive skills embracing both the user and computer disciplines are only available from specialist firms. While this is frequently a successful approach in determining weaknesses, it rarely leads to tangible results in terms of implementation. This is because, unless the personnel concerned have been involved in the fact-gathering and diagnosis, they will rarely be committed to implementation.

Accordingly, the bulk of the diagnostic work should be undertaken by the people within the organisation. This will invariably lead to some priority conflicts with routine work, but given that there is high level policy commitment, this should only prove to be a temporary problem.

At the outset, check-lists should be compiled covering each of the areas of the Total Security Concept:

- Defining a security policy.
- Organisation and procedures.
- Systems security.
- Applications security.
- Physical and fire security.
- Systems, programming and operations standards.
- Personnel practices.
- Insurance.
- Role of internal and external audit.
- Disaster planning and testing.

The compilation of these check-lists can involve an extensive period of time. Such check-lists can also be obtained from independent consultancy firms or from a selected number of books, although the latter do not tend to produce check-lists in easily usable format. The computer suppliers are also producing some worthwhile documentation covering computer security, but once again these do not normally contain check-lists in a practical format.

On balance, the most practical approach is to retain an independent consultant who will make the necessary check-lists available and at the same time be at hand to assist with monitoring progress and contributing appropriate technical expertise. There will also be certain areas which are best reviewed by an independent professional, e.g. personnel practices, standards, etc. These are usually ones where objectivity is difficult for the people within the organisation. The approach is thus for people within the company to do the bulk of the detailed work and for outsiders to contribute concentrated experience and objectivity.

All of the findings should be tabulated in writing and they should be confirmed by the appropriate managers.

The comprehensive review referred to in this section should be undertaken regularly, probally annually or at least every two years. The frequency will depend upon the risk level of applications.

4.   IMPLEMENTING SECURITY MEASURES

It is traditional in the computer environment that the successful outcome of most projects is jeopardised or even eliminated during the implementing phase. The difficulty of planning is its conceptualism; implementation engages the reality of practical issues.

A number of recurrent problems have arisen in the implementation of the Total Security Concept. If any are to be singled out in their importance they are the commitment of management and the dedication of follow-through. These, together with others, are reviewed below:

- Commitment.
- Follow-through.
- Policy.
- Communications.
- Calibre of security management.
- Implementation time lag.
- Priority.
- Costs.

4.1   Commitment

Any management policy requires overt and covert commitment by top management if it is to succeed. Computer security is no exception. Successful projects have all been characterised by the high level of top management commitment coupled with the dedication of the DP professional to ensure that an effective outcome is achieved.

Unfortunately, computer security needs appear to be volatile. A terrorist incident or some form of publicity about abuse raises a perceived need and its priority. This perception is, however, soon eroded by the bustle of day-to-day organisational activities. Management is also reassured by tangible evidence that security is in existence — identity cards and security guards for example.

The vacillating nature of the priority of security must be recognised by management. A failure to do so will soon colour their apparent commitment. This, together with the need for solid follow-through action as described below, is a major problem area.

4.2 Follow-through

The execution of a successful computer security programme will depend largely on the extent to which implementation is under-pinned by a solid action plan. Computer security is not a 'once off' exercise. As reviewed in the initial chapters of this book, it is an on-going exercise. Changes in external environment, many of them surprisingly rapid, and general business priority will all impact on the ability to dedicate resources to the implementation of computer security policies and procedures.

Virtually every computer security programme fails to achieve its deadline for the reasons already outlined. In most instances, these delays are not serious. However, they can become so unless the situation is continually monitored with the view to rescheduling work and ensuring its ultimate implementation.

The computer security committee is an important organisational element in this process. Some organisations have not set up an actual committee but prefer to view matters quarterly or six-monthly at an executive management meeting. The actual method of monitoring the follow-through is not significant. Experience reveals that both methods succeed.

4.3 Policy

Progressive experience with the Total Security Concept has highlighted the fundamental importance of a proper computer security policy as outlined in Chapter 2 of this book. The policy is the precursor to virtually all management action in the area of computer security. If the risks are obscure or are not quantitatively defined, management will attempt to evade real security issues as soon as operational or cost problems emerge.

A large financial institution was constructing a new computer facility. The organisation had defined its risks as high and the losses consequent upon any extended disruption as significant, i.e. in excess of $10,000,000.

The plans for the facility were drawn up to provide protection commensurate with the risks involved. No sooner were they submitted to the contractors than the incoming tenants were subjected to questions, often to the point of ridicule, directed at casting doubt on the measures which had been taken. The organisation had done a good job on its computer security policy. It was then that the value of the work became apparent. It was pointed out to management that either the policy was wrong or the questions being posed by the contractor were out of court. There was little need to debate and the contractor's doubt, which was primarily linked to trust elements on which he had already tendered, was rejected.

4.4   Communications

It is important to communicate accepted policies and procedures all the way down the line to operational staff. There is frequently commitment at the top while the real impact of procedures is felt in the middle and lower levels of staff. Unless adequate effort is given to awareness training and to sound and proper communication much of the good work will be eroded.

A number of organisations have developed cartoon-type caricatures to highlight 'Mister Security'. These, incorporated in posters and featured in monthly or regular house journals, are all aimed at reinforcing the communication process.

Quite often, due to a lack of communication, staff reaction is quite severe. It is frequently said that no sooner has a minimum standard of security been achieved, then staff aver that the organisation is becoming over security-conscious. This is characterised in a form of paranoia where staff feel 'spied' upon. This reaction must be detected as soon as possible. It is an important agenda item for security committee meetings.

4.5   Security Management

The opening chapter of this book reviewed the status of computer security. Specific reference was made to the communications problem between line management and security and computer personnel.

The security function is generally one of the less glamorous ones in management. The top security man rarely reports at top level of management. He is generally an individual with a military or police background and has extreme difficulty in engaging the broader concepts of asset protection, risk management and the new technologies associated with computer security.

There are many aspects of sound computer security which require the involvement and implementation support from security management. Their status in the organisation and perception of security priorities constitutes a major problem in many areas of implementation.

4.6 Elapsed Time to Implementation

Although some benefit can be secured relatively quickly, it is usually found that a broadly based programme takes from nine to twenty-four months to implement. During this period, continuing weaknesses exist, possibly to the extent of a lack of effective disaster recovery plans. Accordingly, the organisation is exposed to material risks during this intervening period.

Experience reveals that it has taken most organisations from nine to eighteen months to survive their first effective disaster recovery test.

4.7 Priority of Security Activities

A good rule of thumb is that the priority assigned to security projects is invariably proportional to the priority of application development activities. This is a primary reason for delays in the implementation of security measures.

This statement certainly reflects the realities of the problem. However, if care is not exercised, it soon becomes a culture. If there is a conflict between the need to implement security work as opposed to application development, security is always the poor relation. Strong follow-through and monitoring of the exercise by management is required if this difficulty is to be avoided. In truth, no security project would ever be implemented if this situation is allowed to continue. Sooner or later, management has to put its foot down and state that certain security activities are equal in priority and importance to the most important non-security activity in hand at the time.

4.8 Costs

Virtually all of the activities outlined are part of policy definition, security procedures and disaster recovery planning and testing, and involve only small implementation costs. There are two exceptions to this rule:

4.8.1 PHYSICAL SECURITY

If physical security facilities are inadequate, it is usually found that extensive alterations are involved in bringing the premises in line with the risks involved. This usually involves extensive costs. In many cases, particularly those of high-risk installations, a completely new facility is required.

A large financial institution had incorporated its computer facility in its corporate headquarters which were housed in a multi-storey building. A view of the physical security demands and features of the site revealed major deficiencies. Not the least of these was the fact that the facility was on the thirteenth floor, one of the intermediary levels of the multi-storey building. Protection of this facility to a level of risk demanded by the potential threat to the organisation was virtually impossible. A short-term action programme was implemented to enhance the existing facility to a point where they would at least offer some protection. The costs involved were approximately $75,000. These enhancements were to ensure a reasonable level of protection while a new computer facility was constructed at a new location.

4.8.2   SYSTEMS AUDITABILITY AND CONTROL

The large computer user had already reached a stage of advancement where large on-line, often real-time, data based supported applications have already been implemented. Most of these have been designed without any real consideration being given to security issues in advance implementation. A typical poor relation area involves restarting back-ups. Little provision also exists for the implementation of a wide range of new auditing techniques such as concurrent processing and integrated test files.

Finally, the design philosophy often incorporates too much centralised emphasis with the inherent risks. Little thought has been given to the decentralisation of the files or data bases. This approach not only yields enhanced effectiveness in many instances but also significantly improves reliability and back-up.

A large computer user with several centralised sites was planning to increase the level of security processing. The basic strategy was to increase terminal intelligence but to retain the philosophy of centralised processing. The concept of intermediate processing between the terminals and the central host had been discarded. However, it was raised again from the security standpoint. By that time, new information processing and projected volumes was available. After appropriate evaluation, a decision was taken to develop the company's systems with the intermediary level. There was no additional cost involved, but had a decision been taken to change strategy in this way at a later stage, significant costs would have been involved in implementing the revised approach.

4.8.3   EXISTING APPLICATIONS

It is often found that existing applications fail to meet the objective contained within a security policy in terms of control, processing philosophies, etc. Significant cost can be involved in remedying these deficiencies.

A large computer user with a major on-line inventory control system with national coverage confirmed significant weaknesses in the design concept of its system from a security point of view. After an evaluation, it was discovered that nearly sixty man-years of effort would be required to redesign the system which could not be modified easily to meet security demands.

5. COMPILE AN ACTION PLAN

There will be certain areas where security effectiveness is deficient and action is required immediately. These will generally be in areas of high risk or where the impact on the organisation is significant. Others can be undertaken at a more leisurely pace and implemented over a more protracted period. Accordingly, the action plan should be divided into two parts:

1. Short-term action to be implemented within a three-month period.
2. Medium-to-long-term action implemented in three to twelve months.

In each case, priorities should be carefully reviewed, task lists broken down into as much detail as possible in order to get a proper measure of the work to be implemented, and responsibility clearly assigned.

All of the action items should be clearly cost-justified, as described in Chapter 2, in order to facilitate decision-taking.

6. DISASTER PLANNING AND TESTS

An important function of the security committee is the planning and holding of disaster tests. The procedures have been reviewed in detail in Chapter 11.

7. LONG-RANGE COMPUTER PLANNING AND SECURITY

On several occasions in this book reference has been made to the increasing scale and complexity of computer applications. So has the fact that most applications primarily have business rather than security objectives.

Most of these difficulties can be pre-empted by considering computer security during the initial stages of long-range computer planning. It is at this stage that the foundations for computer effectiveness are structured and security effectiveness is an important part of computer effectiveness.

Long-range computer plans should be carefully perused and analysed by the security committee. Any special security implications should be highlighted and appropriate action taken.

8. SUMMARY

Effective computer security is best achieved by the creation of a computer security committee which contains representatives from all appropriate functions. The committee will assume responsibility for co-ordinating the review of computer security on a regular and surprise basis, and for the implementation of appropriate action. The holding of regular meetings by the security committee ensures regular monitoring of activities and that the priority of computer security is not depreciated over the passage of time.

APPENDIX 1

Computer Security Risk Inventory

	Key Issue Yes/No	Adequate Yes/No
Security Policy		
A defined security policy exists		
Responsibility for policy formulation assigned		
Senior management awareness and commitment		
Scope of loss has been defined		
Organisation and Division of Responsibility		
Responsibility for security assigned		
Clear job descriptions		
Inclusion of security in job descriptions		
Division of responsibility between key functions		
Well defined systems of internal check		
Systems Security		
Hardware trapdoors defined		
Software trapdoors defined		
Terminal security		
Network security		
Back-up		
Applications Security		
User controls		
DP controls		
Application contingency plans		
Data and file security		
Physical Security		
Access to personnel		
Burglar alarms		
Location		
Construction		
Layout		

	Key Issue Yes/No	Adequate Yes/No
Fire Security		
Fire detection		
Fire fighting		
Fire department liaison		
Fire drill		
Standards		
Methods and supervision		
Documentation		
Back-up duplicates		
Personnel Practices		
Recruitment practices		
Performance appraisals		
Leave		
Job rotation		
Insurance		
Hardware		
Software		
Personnel		
Loss of profits		
Audit		
Skills		
Specialised techniques		
Liaison with systems development		
Role clarity		

APPENDIX 2

Computer Security Review

Company ....

Prepared by ....

Date...

1. Division of Responsibilities	Reply	Acceptable	Further Review Needed
1.1. To whom is the data processing department responsible?			
1.2. Are there separate units in the department for each of the following? If so, indicate the unit manager/supervisor and describe their responsibilities:			
a. development;			
b. data preparation;			
c. computer operation;			
d. file library;			
e. data control.			
1.3. Has an organisation chart been prepared? If so, attach a copy and cross reference the answers in 1.2. above to it.			
1.4. Describe the steps that have been taken to ensure adequate succession in respect of key personnel, e.g. data processing manager, systems manager, operations manager.			
1.5. Show on the organisation chart just how this will be achieved.			
1.6. Do all personnel know about this plan?			
1.7. Do the following basic restrictions apply? Indicate in each case how the restriction is enforced:			
a. access to documents containing original data is limited to the data preparation and the control section staff;			

	Reply	Acceptable	Further Review Needed
b. access to the computer during production runs is limited to computer operators;			
c. access to current files and programs is limited to computer operators;			
d. computer operators and programmers do not amend input data and do not have unrestricted access to punch rooms;			
e. control section staff do not have other duties within data processing departments;			
f. computer department staff cannot initiate transactions or changes to master files;			
g. unauthorised access to the computer room is forbidden (state who is authorised and their position in the company).			
1.8. Do the restrictions in questions 1.7. apply outside normal working hours? If so, how are they enforced? If not, which ones are not enforced?			

APPENDIX 3

Computer Security Review
Extract of Checklist on Evidential Checks

Company ....

Prepared by ....

Date...

2. Control over Operators/Equipment	Reply	Acceptable	Further Review Needed
2.5. Are computer usage reports examined:			
a. to check operators' performance and machine efficiency?			
b. does the examination include a check to ensure that all runs carried out for users are being properly charged?			
c. are charges rendered to users cross-referenced to the usage report?			
d. how often is this examination carried out?			
e. by whom is it carried out (indicate name and position)?			
f. how is this examination evidenced?			

APPENDIX 4

CASE STUDY: COMPUTER SECURITY IN A SMALL INSTALLATION

1. BACKGROUND

The company is the subsidiary of a large multi-national manufacturing and distributing firm specialising in heavy transport and excavation equipment. The basic nature of the company's operations is the import and maintenance of the equipment. There is a limited local content assembly programme using components and parts imported CKD from the American parent.

The company employs a staff of several hundred in its operations. The basic activity is the repair and maintenance of equipment in the field. A large store of parts is maintained to provide the necessary back up support to users.

The company has a System 34 mini computer. This is primarily used for an inventory control application. There are related costing applications as well as a comprehensive set of accounting and financial systems.

Initially, the data processing department comprised a manager and one operator. However, the data processing manager left after the initial applications were mounted and the company experienced extreme difficulty in supporting its applications. Subsequently, a data processing manager was recruited who also undertook the bulk of the systems analysis and design work. He built up the staff of the department to a team of two programmers and two operators.

2. APPROACH TO COMPUTER SECURITY

After the departure of the DP manager, the company was in a quandary. Security and controls generally were non-existent. Application work was processed late and contained numerous inaccuracies. There was no documentation for any of the computer systems. A firm of consultants was called in to run the installation on a facilities management basis. They did this with difficulty due to the lack of documentation and poorly designed systems. Subsequently, a management decision was taken to view the department afresh and a new DP manager was recruited. He was given full management support to rehabilitate the installation.

The remainder of this section reviews the security action taken in regard to the Total Computer Security Concept.

2.1 Organisation and Division of Responsibility

This is always difficult in a small department. The managing director of the company agreed to assume overall responsibility for computer security. He delegated this responsibility to the line managers who had accountability for the various applications.

Technical responsibility for computer security was assigned to the data processing manager. He defined a range of standards and procedures embracing the various technical areas under his control.

A control clerk was recruited with overall responsibility for off-line scheduling and monitoring of work flow. In addition, all controlled responsibilities were handled by this individual. These activities were taken away from the operators who had previously performed them. Programmers were not permitted to operate computer systems thereby further reinforcing divisions of responsibility.

2.2 Systems Security

A further analysis was undertaken with the computer supplier of the required level of systems security, features in the operating system which contributed to security, and various hardware standards which needed to be enforced. Arising out of this, a series of standard practices was compiled and issued to the programmers and operators.

As the company had certain on-line applications, user procedures and practices were also embraced by this study.

2.3 Physical Security

This had been non-existent. There was free access to the computer room and to related magnetic media and documentation. At virtually no cost, certain doors were locked and access was restricted through one door. The external window was protected with film and adequate burglar proofing. A burglar alarm system was installed to monitor after hours activity.

A suitable fire-proof safe was installed in the computer room for the disc packs being maintained there. Copies were taken of the systems, programming and operations documentation and these were stored in a fire-proof safe at a second site. A system was implemented for rotating input data and master files and back up copies of these were stored at a remote location.

2.4 Fire Security

A fire contingency and evacuation procedure was compiled and all affected staff were trained in it. As it is a small installation, it was considered that hand-held extinguishers would be adequate and a suitable quantity of these were procured for use both inside the computer room and within its proximity. Fire detectors were installed for monitoring after hours situations with a direct line to the security officer.

2.5   Applications Security

Controls were reviewed and established in the user areas to ensure that all transaction and master file data were submitted and processed in a complete and accurate form. These controls were reconciled with the controls kept by the computer department.

As already mentioned, back up copies of transactions, master files are stored at a remote location.

2.6   Standards

A set of standards for systems, programming and operations activities has now been compiled and is in full use. This covers methods and documentation standards. A complete series of check points has been established in order to ensure adequate hand-overs between the user and the computer department and amongst computer staff themselves.

The use of structured techniques is being incorporated in the systems and programming standards. This has helped the development of systems in a way that there is no undue dependence on any staff member. Furthermore, the use of walk-throughs has facilitated quality control and documentation.

A procedure for change control over operational systems exists and is rigorously monitored by the control clerk and the DP manager. Finally, comprehensive standards have been compiled for the stratified testing and acceptance of new systems or modifications thereto. The user participates extensively in these tests.

2.7   Personnel Practices

Performance appraisals takes place every six months. These have been modified to evaluate the attitude of computer staff so that any negative aspects or demotivation is detected.

Whereas in the past personnel had not been thoroughly reference-checked, this procedure has now been changed. The personnel department participates extensively in recruitment and undertakes the reference checking work.

2.8   Insurance

An annual review of the insurance of the computer resources takes place. In the past, there have been no adequate insurance against disruption or the reconstruction of destroyed information. This has been remedied by incorporation of these risks into the company's loss of profits policy.

2.9   Audit Role

The company does not have its own internal audit staff. Accordingly, extensive discussions were held between the financial director and external auditors after which it was agreed that the external auditors would extend their normal range of checks in the computer area. A series of audit objectives were defined by the management in conjunction with their auditors. Auditors participate in important checkpoints during the systems development or modification of systems. They also make use of generalised audit software for the stratification of data and files and statistical sampling of processing.

Finally, they undertake a comprehensive review of the control records against the production documentation with a view to identifying any discrepancies.

3. CONCLUSION

There were no major problems encountered in the course of implementing this scheme. The only conflict experienced was between the need to use staff for operational work as opposed to dedicating them exclusively to the security project.

3.1 Costs and Time

The cost of implementing the scheme, exclusive of the time expended by the staff of the client, was £3,000. The total time involved in implementing it was just over two months.

APPENDIX 5

Glossary of Computer Terms

A.

Audit — the steps devised to confirm evidence relating to the authenticity and validity of data in a data processing system.

C.

Control — a function built into a program as a checking mechanism.

Conversion program — a program designed to convert data from one form to another eg the language of one machine to that of another.

D.

Data — In computer terminology — facts, information or characters processed, stored or produced by computer.

Data base — a shared collection of inter-related data designed to meet the needs of many types of user.

Data capture — the obtaining of data by means of a device which can communicate with a computer system.

Data preparation — recording data by means of an input medium in preparation for input to a computer.

Data processing (DP) — the arranging of data into a form suited to producing required results; the handling of data in order to classify, sort, calculate and record; and the production and updating of records and reports.

Disc — a thin circular plate covered by magnetic material on which data is recorded and stored. Discs are essentially of two types: hard and floppy. Hard discs have a base of metal or glass. The floppy variety are plastic based.

Documentation — a description of the functions of a program or set of programs or a system.

F.

File — a collection of data on one or more related topics which is handled as a single entity.

H.

Hardware — data processing equipment including a computer system — mainframe, mini or micro — and peripheral equipment, such as terminals and line-printers.

Hard-copy — computer output in permanent form, usually a print-out on continuous stationery.

I.

Interface — the point of interaction between two systems or processes.

L.

Librarian function — the program that maintains and gives access to the programs, routines and data which constitute an operating system. Such functions can include system generation and editing.

M.

Magnetic tape — tape or ribbon coated with magnetic material on which information can be stored. It is a sequential storage medium and for this reason large delays can be experienced in accessing data.

Master data — data which is rarely changed and provides basic information for processing operations. The term also refers to the content of a master file.

Master file — a file, the contents of which are stable and rarely changed. It normally provides information for a specified process.

Mainframe — a word used to describe a large computer. It relates to the essential part of the machine which contains the central processing unit (CPU) and the control mechanism of a computer system.

Mini-computer — a machine smaller in both size, power and cost than a mainframe computer.

Micro-computer — a small machine built around a microprocessor having input and output facilities and a memory.

O.

Operators — people who operate a computer and its systems.

P.

Program — a series of instructions to tell a computer how to perform a specific task.

Programmer — a person who develops or codes computer programs using a programming language.

R.

Routine — a set of instructions which enable a computer to perform a clearly defined task.

S.

Software — a generic term for programs, including both applications programs, (eg payroll, debtors) and systems programs, (eg operating systems and compilers).

Systems analyst — a person skilled in problem definition and analysis who examines a business or industrial situation and designs a computer system to meet its information and operations needs.

Software support system — a system designed to assist the programmer to develop and check out the correct functioning of a program.

T.

Terminal — This is the means by which a user communicates with a computer. It is an input/output device and typically consists of a keyboard, screen and/or a printer. It may also incorporate a microprocessor and programming facilities.

APPENDIX 6

Further Reading

1. **Computer Security: A Management Audit Approach**
   Norman L Enger and Paul W Howerton
   AMACOM, 1980
   ISBN 0 8144 5582 4

2. **Computer Fraud and Countermeasures**
   Leonard I Krauss and Aileen MacGahan
   Prentice Hall, 1979
   ISBN 0 13 164772 5

3. **Computer Control Guidelines**
   Canadian Institute of Chartered Accountants, 1977
   ISBN 0 88800 032 4

4. **Contingency Planning**
   D Broadbent
   NCC Publications, 1979
   ISBN 0 85012 192 2

5. **Computer Security: the Personnel Aspect**
   T Squires
   NCC Publications, 1980
   ISBN 0 85012 246 5

6. **Computer Security: Risk Analysis and Control**
   K K Wong
   NCC Publications, 1977
   ISBN 0 85012 179 5